The Human Being as Music

by Lea van der Pals

Translated by Alan Stott from the second German edition

Der Mensch Musik

The Robinswood Press

Stourbridge England

© Philosophisch-Anthroposphischer Verlag am Goetheanum

Dornach   Switzerland

1969 and 1981

This Translation © Alan Stott 1992

The Robinswood Press
Stourbridge   England

ISBN 1 869981 46 4

Support for this publication from Lea van der Pals is gratefully acknowledged.

All Rights reserved. No part of this publication may be reproduced, stored in a retrieval system, or transmitted, in any form, or by any means, electronic, mechanical, photocopying, recording or otherwise, without the prior permission in writing from the publisher.

Typeset by Wynstones Press Gloucester
Printed and bound in Great Britain by Billings and Sons Ltd Worcester

CONTENTS

Introduction to the English Edition	1
Preface to the Second German Edition	9
Foreword	10
Introduction	11
Cosmic Music	14
The Human Being and Music	16
Music as 'Human Being'	17
'The Human Being as Music'	18
Necessity and Freedom	21
Centre and Periphery	
That which exists (The Note)	23
That which is active (The Interval)	25
The Realm of the Heart: Major and Minor	29
The Threefold 'Human Being as Music'	33
'To grasp the musical element, we have to enter into the spiritual realm'	37
'Living with the gods'	43
Sources and Notes	46
Further Reading	75
Bibliographic Survey	76

Introduction to the English Edition

As students of language we can notice changes occurring over recent decades in the use of such words as *music, musician, composer, expression, creativity,* and so on. Splintering of meaning is now far advanced. Different groups of professional people use the same words for widely different activities and pursuits, stemming from different conceptions and preconceptions. [1]

Jazz, pop and 'folk' music, the synthesizer, the recording industry have all developed their own techniques and jargon in catering to the demands of large sections of the population. The call for a drastic reassessment of the curriculum and examination requirements by educationalists advocating a broader teaching of techniques, is one attempt to bridge the gaps dividing musical practice today. This should prepare music pupils for their future tasks in a world largely geared to the entertainment industry. Professional composers themselves are largely subject to demands and expectations. Probably few ivory towers exist nowadays. 'Originality' is often seen in terms of exploiting instrumental technique to the limits, or the exploring of new possibilities of electronically produced sound. Scores of unbelievable complexity are initially appreciated by only a handful of sophisticated people. Of course, the need for technique and standards as an essential part of artistic integrity is not gainsaid. In this complex musical situation, reactions of the musical public vary from excitement and fascination to boredom and rejection.

Anthroposophical musicians have offered comments on the modern musical scene. Reubke [2] describes on the one hand 'musical intellectualism' and on the other 'musical psychism'. Is there a path between these extremes? Pfrogner spent many years researching twentieth century developments, and produced standard books on the subject.[3] His categories are based on his analysis of sound: he makes a distinction between *Tonkern, Klanghülle, and Schallhülle,* which we might translate as 'musical essence', 'mantle of sound' or 'resonance', and 'acoustic reverberation'. For Pfrogner there is an 'art of music', an 'art of sound' and bare-faced 'art of noise', in the world today.

To the ordinary person, sensing the mood of the 'nineties, it might appear that we have *all* become 'artists'. Every entertainer is now 'creative', every child 'composes' as part of the examination requirements, everyone must have his 'self-expression' and relaxation through 'music'. In all this, how much is *real*, how much a caricature? How long, for example, will the pressing of buttons on electrical sound sources pass for a fulfilling of *fundamental* human needs of the soul? Amidst the din assaulting our senses today, are there signs that a sufficient number of people are taking the time to ask what is happening to the word MUSIC? The decisive question is whether the path of *actively* participating through listening is being pursued. In the world today, how much is the past masquerading in another guise, but basically untransformed? Today we not only have the future of the planet to consider, but also the future of mankind! Matching the conflicts without, there are the conflicts facing every composer as he writes, conflicts in every classroom, every practice room and every church and concert hall. Today it is no longer enough to claim with Rossini that two types of music exist, 'the good and the bad'. We are faced with the question at every stage: What is living music and where is it being fostered? This is beyond 'what feels great', beyond 'keeping music live': it is a question of *human consciousness* and the *musical raw material*.

With notable exceptions, musicians (no doubt engrossed in the task of making music) have generally been slow to acknowledge Steiner's contributions on the subject. And his followers, too, have generally been slow to realize the other side of the question, why Steiner himself, active in the other arts, was apparently not directly creative in music. It is true that he did not write symphonies, but we can discover where Steiner channelled his musicality. He poured it into his work as a teacher of humanity:

> It gave me particular pleasure to be told one day by one of our artistically gifted friends that some of the lecture cycles I have given could be transcribed into symphonies purely on the basis of their inner structure. Some of the courses are indeed based in their structure on something very like this. Take, for instance, the cycle given in Vienna on the life between death and a new birth, and you will see that you could make a symphony out of it. [4]

The task of discovering this music, the flow in and behind the structure of the spoken and written word, is an exacting one. For it appeals to the engaged will, which lies deeper than the mere understanding. This fact underlies the true nature of anthroposophy, which is not an intellectual system but a living movement for cultural renewal.

> For anyone who would read my *Occult Science* as today he would read a novel or another book, passively giving himself to it, it is really only a thicket of words — and so are my other books. It is only someone who, in every moment of reading, knows that he has to create out of the depths of his own soul, and through his most intimate willing (something for which the books should be the stimulus), only this person is able to regard these books as musical scores out of which he can gain the experience in his own soul of the true piece of music. This active experience of the soul of the individual, however, is what is needed.[5]

In revealing sentences, Steiner links the central 'art of the ego', music, with spiritual striving.

> But the human being is able long, long before he consciously finds himself in all that I have described as the stages of the path of initiation, to express these stages through the means at his disposal, in evocative images, and this occurs through the language of music. In the final analysis, in the essentials, true music is the progressive, developing drama of existence in the medium of sounds, which are an external image of what the soul lives through consciously in the life of initiation. [6]

There can be no doubt that Steiner became a complete artist, who matched his earlier achievements in philosophy and science. He repeatedly emphasized the need for spiritual research to lead over into artistic activity. He recognized Wagner's aim to create a *Gesamtkunstwerk*, a complete work of art, and spoke of the attempt in *Parsifal* to pioneer a modern mystery art.[7] The First Goetheanum was Steiner's own attempt to establish a centre where all the arts could flourish. It was a 'living Word'. [8] The Word, as Lea van der Pals points out, includes Music. For the First Goetheanum, that remarkable, all-wooden building, 'was musical... was eurythmical'. [9] As Lea van der Pals also points out, the arts were to rediscover their source in the new mysteries which would lead them to a renewed future. Eurythmy, a transformation and culmination of all the arts, was born. [10] Eurythmists have the task of fashioning gesture to reveal the *human* content of soul and spirit. Steiner explains:

> If... someone feels that here on earth he does not fulfil what lies in his archetype, with its abode in the heavens, then there arises in him an artistic longing for some outer image of that archetype. Whereupon he can gain the power to become an instrument for expressing the true relation of man to the world by becoming a eurythmist. The eurythmist says: All the movements which I ordinarily carry out here on earth do less than justice to the mobile archetype of man. To present the ideal human archetype I must begin by finding a way to unite myself with its movements. These movements, through which the human being endeavours to imitate in space the movements of his heavenly archetype, constitute eurythmy... which is neither indicative nor sweeping, but *expressive* gesture. [11]

To be truly contemporary, and not simply fashionable, artists (players and eurythmists) strive to *express* through the language of beauty the soul and spirit in the music, whether it is by Bach, Beethoven or Britten. This is what speaks across the years 'from the heart to the heart', as Beethoven put it, and this is why people go to concerts. 'Music,' said Vaughan Williams, 'is a reaching out to the ultimate realities by means of ordered sound.' The recreative artist also seeks the composer's source of inspiration, which is more than a question of 'style'. Here we can link up to the earlier question of the nature of living music. For eurythmy can provide an acid test: what is *abstractly* conceived is unable to find a *concrete*, artistic expression. (Hence the tragedy of Hauer, as Steiner points out in his lecture course on music eurythmy, lecture five, 23.2.24.) And the other extreme, an improvisatory, instinctive 'art of sound' exciting emotional states, can also offer little material for eurythmy, however sensitive the musicians. It is also self-evident that electronics disappears from view, too.

As Pfrogner insists, to find answers to all the musical questions, experiments and researches of our century, including the question whether the diatonic system (that 'image of the human being, pure and simple') has a *future*, we are referred to the musicality of human beings themselves. Eurythmy, an art that reveals musicality, has a tremendous contribution to make. [12] But there are no *formulae*. Living answers to today's challenges will have to be found by everyone, individually. As Reubke puts it:

> Musical experience is not experience of the past and not experience of the future, but has the character of the universal present. Musical sound is neither a picture of something nor something ideal, nor does it serve a purpose for something. Musical sound is the appearance in the sensory world of the soul's presence within human consciousness. [13]

The concepts of transformation and rediscovery are likely to be supremely relevant today and in the future. Do we *still* believe that machines will help us achieve inner listening? Perhaps Beethoven's personal destiny is a picture for all modern aspiration: the more Beethoven's outer ear failed him, the more his 'inner ear' developed. Pfrogner insists that only inner, active listening will guarantee a future for the art of music. Inner work precedes and accompanies the outer work. On the way it will be confirmed that artistic 'theory', to which the present book is a contribution, is intensely concrete, and furthermore, artists involved in real 'conflicts' and 'suffering' should not lose sight of what can flow from their art to a humanity in need. Steiner sums up:

> The fact that materialism holds sway over our age is, really, only a lagging behind. Man only became an earth citizen in the Greek age: today he is already so estranged from his earth citizenship he no longer understands how to handle his soul-spirit being in relation to his body — it is one of the requirements of the age for the human being to perceive spirit and soul in himself without the physical element... We have to overcome hostility towards development; must open ourselves to it. Then we shall acquire a quite natural relationship to anthroposophical

growth of spirit and pass over from antiquated needs to the truly modern need of mankind: namely, to raise ourselves to the spiritual realm. [14] The present translation of *Der Mensch MUSIK* attempts to convey the meaning of the original German in English as used in England. We have tried to tackle problems afresh, from a background of working for many years in eurythmy and music.

Some details of our translation may surprise some readers, though we have considered alternatives and asked for help in order to achieve the most accurate version of the texts. A brief discussion of a single word may interest the reader, not only to illustrate a problem, but even to indicate a practical means to overcome it. Let us take the word *Ton*, German for 'note'. English musicians play 'notes'; German musicians *Töne*. *Ton* is used as a prefix in *Tonkunst*, the art of music; *Tonhöhe*, pitch; *Tonfarbe*, timbre or tone-colour, and so on. The German *Noten* is our (sheet) music. *Ton* is also used for mood, as in *klagender Ton*, lamenting mood. Goethe uses *Durton* and *Mollton* (footnote 20) for major and minor moods. English 'tone,' apart from meaning two semitones, is a quality of sound - a player has a 'good tone' or a 'rich tone', which then links to extra-musical usage, as 'tone of voice', 'tone control' on tape decks; we even speak of 'tones of colour'. American musicians talk about 'tones', as in 'tone-row'; a tone is what sounds, but they play 'notes' too. For them 'notes' can also mean sheet-music as well (as in German). It might be thought that English *poets* prefer to hear or imagine 'tones', though Shakespeare's Don Pedro advises 'do it in notes', and Titania begs 'I pray you gentle mortal, sing again Mine ear is much enamoured of thy note', and Arviragus says: 'use like note, and words, Save that Euriphide must be Fidele'. Shelley, too, in his *'Music'*:

> I pant for the music which is divine
> My heart in its thirst is a dying flower;
> Pour forth the sound like enchanted wine,
> Loosen the notes in a silver shower...

Should it be 'tone' for the music of the spheres and 'note' for music on earth? [15] Steiner uses *Ton* for both. The correct term in the USA would be 'tone' in most, though not all, cases. If *Laut* (sound) is correctly translated as 'speech' in 'speech eurythmy', an internationally acceptable solution might be to translate *Ton* (also 'sound' here) as 'music', in 'music eurythmy'. Then people would have no doubt that eurythmy is 'visible music', or, more correctly, 'visible singing', and not something else. Whatever happens to composers, players, eurythmists and audience in the world of sleep, on the earth they all practise the art of music. Steiner, incidentally, uses the expression *musikalisches Eurythmisieren*, literally 'musical eurythmizing', in lecture 7 of the 1924 course. In our translation of *Ton* we have usually employed 'note', sometimes 'sound', 'musical sound' or 'music', and the adjective 'tonal'.

What's in a word, someone might ask? Well, could clarification of terms perhaps be the first stage in really living the difference between speech and music eurythmy (see footnote 37)? Moreover, to go to the heart of the matter, if there were an English word for *Ansatz* would there be less risk of confusing the movements for speech and those for music? Brass players speak of 'attack' which is shorter than 'point of departure', certainly. Perhaps several alternatives, like 'onset', 'inception' and 'origin' would serve the purpose, or the verb 'initiate' — in plain Anglo-Saxon 'begin'. While we are about it, even in the German *Schwung* (literally: 'swing' or 'leap'), another fundamental activity, the almost simultaneous 'release' and fresh 'attack', is not sufficiently conveyed. In English, 'break' or 'breath' might serve as long as the ensuing 'attack' is not forgotten. But here we are encroaching into technical matters.

This translation has been made in a spirit of gratitude for the work of Lea van der Pals, which we personally have come to know for the most part through her colleagues and pupils. Her study, distilling as it does a lifetime's devotion, may yet help to inspire artistic life to new heights. For in the last resort it matters less where eurythmists are trained than whether they have found the artistic source in speech and in music. The translators are certainly not the first to suggest that the way forward in human terms is to work with speaker and musician for a true reconciliation of the arts as Rudolf Steiner intended — even if one is 'only' translating!

Our grateful thanks go especially to Margaret Miles, Robin Cook, Johanna Collis and Dr David Rycroft who all read the typescript and made valuable suggestions.

Ashurst Wood, Michaelmas 1991   Alan Stott
                                         Maren Weissenborn

> From Harmony, from heavenly Harmony
> This universal frame began;
> From harmony to harmony
> Through all the compass of the notes it ran,
> The diapason closing full in Man.
>
> from Song for St. Cecilia's Day, 1687
>
>   John Dryden

REFERENCES

1. Hermann Pfrogner, 'Der Zerrissene Orpheus. Von der Dreigliederung zur Dreiteilung der Musik: Tonalität − Atonalität − Elektronik' (1957), reprinted in Pfrogner Zeitwende der Musik, Langen Müller: München/Wien 1986. (Translation in manuscript 'Orpheus dismembered, from the threefold nature of music to its division into three parts: tonality - atonality - electronics', in 'Music's turning-point of time'.) See also Steiner, Knowledge of the Higher Worlds − how is it Achieved? chap VII 'The splitting of the human personality during spiritual training', RSP London, and AP New York. GA 10.

   Chr. Peter finds this experience portrayed in the march accompanying the trials in Mozart's Magic Flute: 'What a strange picture appears before us! Not only the singular instrumentation (the strings with their expressive soul are missing) but above all the division of the three realms of melody, harmony and rhythm, which, as we discussed above, correspond to the three soul-forces of thinking, feeling and willing, cause us to hold our breath. The division of the soul-forces is something, which, according to Steiner, occurs in the life after death and consequently belongs to the strangeness of the path of initiation, too. In our own age which itself stands on the threshold, such a division is no longer quite incomprehensible.' Chr. Peter: Die Sprache der Musik in Mozarts 'Zauberflöte', Verlag Freies Geistesleben, Stuttgart 1983 (Translation in manuscript 'The Language of music in Mozart's Magic Flute'). See also Goethe's Fairy-Tale and Steiner's Mystery Dramas.

2. Lothar Reubke, Introduction to H.Beckh, Die Sprache der Tonart, Urachhaus, Stuttgart 1977. (Translation in manuscript 'The language of tonality'.)

3. Pfrogner, ibid., and Lebendige Tonwelt (Translation in manuscript 'The living world of music'), Langen Müller: München/Wien, 2nd edition 1981.

4. Steiner, Practical Course for Teachers (lecture Stuttgart 21.8.19) GA 294. The lecture course referred to is GA 153, The Inner Nature of Man and the Life between Death and a New Birth, 2nd ed. RSP, London, 1959.

   See reference to Old Saturn in Eurythmy as Visible Music, forthcoming third edition: Eurythmy as Visible Singing, lecture 6, 25.2.24.

   An extensive discussion of Steiner's point forms Chapter 4 of E. Schwebsch, J.S.Bach und die Kunst der Fuge, Freies Geistesleben, Stuttgart, third edition 1988. 'The cosmology of Occult Science contains in its thoughts the best exercises for a meditative musician who is searching for new forms today' (p.211). Schwebsch's chapter also contains a justification for music eurythmy which is unlikely to be superseded.

5. Steiner, Heilfaktoren für den sozialen Organismus, (lecture Dornach, 2.7.20). GA 198.

6. Steiner, Art as seen in the Light of Mystery Wisdom, (lecture Dornach, 30.12.14) RSP London 1984. GA 275. See Steiner: 'Music today has reached lofty heights in its historical, global development, but the musical element is contaminated today by everything else experienced in this materialistic age. Yet by virtue of the pure musical element people today could not fail to be anthroposophists. If you want seriously to research the musical element you will find it cannot be experienced

other than anthroposophically.' Lecture, Stuttgart 8.3.23 in *The Inner nature of Music*, AP, New York. (Observations follow on the writing of a passage concerning the ninefold nature of the human being in the book *Theosophy*.) Steiner himself was able to make the above claims because for him the richness of initiation knowledge was a living experience. He hoped his followers would progress beyond an intellectual level of enquiry to Imagination and even Inspiration, which is directly musical. Composers should be 'most significantly stimulated' (30.12.14). The paragraph quoted above (which should be read in context) is often interpreted to mean that musicians are, in a way, already anthroposophists, which to some extent could apply, but is perhaps a dangerous claim if pressed too far. Great performers are often mentioned, whose musicality exhibits a spirituality – for example Yehudi Menuhin, Furtwängler, Bruno Walter (who publicly acknowledged his debt to Steiner in *Music and Music-Making*, Faber, London 1953). What Edwin Fischer said of Mozart could be a stimulation in this regard: 'What raised Mozart to the highest stage of spiritual maturity which it is possible for an earthly being to reach, was the art of moderation, of only indicating – this "playing" with the great human passions and also leaving a space to experience the divine light which is in each of us whether already comprehended or only dimly felt. Hence the difficulty of performing his music, despite the simplicity of the outer garment. He really did surmount the earthly, not only through grace and miracle as people think, but through spiritual work on himself and his art. What occurs is not so important, if only the heart lights up in sorrow and joy... Mozart is not sweetness, is not *aesthetic*. Mozart is the touchstone of the heart; through him we are able to protect ourselves from all the illnesses of taste, of mind, of the feelings – here speaks a simple, noble, healthy and open, purified human heart within the divine language of music' (Edwin Fischer, *Musikalische Betrachtungen*, Wiesbaden, 1956).

7 'Christianity will permeate art, will broaden and inspire it, will bestow in abundance the power of artistic creation. Wagner's *Parsifal* is the first foreshadowing of this.' Steiner, 'Easter: the Mystery of the Future' (lecture Berlin, 13.4.08) in Steiner, *The Festivals and their Meaning* RSP London 1981. See also Steiner: 'Die Musik des Parsifal als Ausdruck des Uebersinnlichen' lecture Kassel, 16.01.07, in *Das Christliche Mysterium*. GA 97.

8 Steiner, *Ways to a New Style in Architecture* (lecture Dornach 7.6.14). GA 286.

9 Steiner, *Eurythmy as Visible Music* (forthcoming third edition, *Eurythmy as Visible Singing*), (lecture Dornach 23.2.24). GA 278.

10 See Steiner *Art as seen in the light of Mystery Wisdom* (lecture Dornach 29.12.14) RSP London. 1984. GA 275.

11 Steiner, *The Arts and their Mission* (lecture Dornach 27.5.23) AP New York. GA 276.

12 The valuable articles of the early eurythmist-musician Ralph Kux (1903-1965) first appeared in *Das Goetheanum*. In 'Eurythmy and Music' (1945), he concludes with a far-reaching vision of a future possibility:

'Steiner traced the musical element right back to the human being himself. He recognised that music can solely appear with the human being. By creating a new image of wisdom for the human being in anthroposophy, he transfigured at the same time the musical essence of the human being. He brought this musical essence into visibility in music eurythmy, and therewith at the same time gave the musician the possibility, through a new artistic medium, to carry music on to a new level of consciousness, to a new resurrection. Spiritual knowledge of the human being must again become "a musical knowledge, a vital knowledge of the elements of music".' (Steiner, *Das tonerlebnis im Menschen*, GA 283 (*The Inner Nature of Music and the Experience of Tone*, AP, New York, 1983.)) Ralph Kux: see 'further reading' below.

13 Reubke, op.cit.

14 Steiner, *The Arts and their Mission* (lecture Dornach 27.5.23) AP New York. GA 276.

15 Shelley's translation 'from the Faust of Goethe' of '*Die Sonne tönt nach alter Weise/In Brudersphären Wettgesang...*' runs 'The sun makes music as of old/Amid the rival spheres of Heaven...' In a footnote he adds 'a literal translation of this astonishing Chorus': 'The sun sounds, according to ancient custom. In the song of emulation of his brother-spheres...' Shelley adds 'it is impossible to represent in another language the melody of the versification; even the volatile strength and delicacy of the ideas escape in the crucible of translation, and the reader is surprised to find a *caput mortuum*'. This is surely an understatement from a gifted translator!

Key to Abbreviations

AP — Anthroposophic Press
RSP — Rudolf Steiner Press
GA — Gesamtausgabe, complete edition of Steiner's works
(see Bibliographic Survey)

Preface to the Second German Edition

When the book *Der Mensch — MUSIC* appeared twelve years ago, this summary of the statements of Rudolf Steiner on the essence and effects of music met a real need. Musicians and eurythmists have found in it stimulation and points of view with which they could enrich and deepen their work. Despite further important publications in this domain which have meanwhile appeared, I have resisted changing the text for this second edition. The original structure remains untouched.

In order to help the reader in the search for the quotations from the works of Rudolf Steiner, the Appendix has been extended. I would like to express my warm thanks to the publisher for the editor's valuable help with this section.

Dornach, Whitsun 1981   Lea van der Pals

Foreword

Rudolf Steiner gave new suggestions out of anthroposophy for all artistic activity. As the arts were in danger of losing their way in the materialism and intellectual aridity of most cultural life, he wished to give them a fresh start based on the perceptions of anthroposophy. From these perceptions the arts could be renewed and fructified by a new consciousness. In this lay the new idea, which was unheard of up to then, that artists could now consciously travel on a path of practising without departing from the realm of art, that they could learn consciously to immerse themselves into a spiritually deepened experience without being caught up in abstract notions.

Steiner not only gave suggestions and indications for the different arts but he was himself an active exponent in all of them except music. It has often been said that what he gave for music was much less 'new' than for the other arts. Was this because music appeared less immediately in danger from the decline of culture apparent in the first quarter of our century? It has since then suffered its 'fall' all the more rapidly and more radically. Notwithstanding, Steiner did take precautions. A thread of wonderful and most illuminating indications on the nature and effect of the musical element traverses the whole of his lecturing activity. The peak is the lecture course on *music eurythmy* of February 1924: *Eurythmy as Visible Singing*. Here Steiner created a musical instrument, namely the eurythmically motivated human being. This is the adequate instrument for the 'most human' art, music. In it the human being is at the same time instrument and player.

The attempt is made in what follows to trace Steiner's widely interspersed indications on the musical element and with the help of aspects of music eurythmy to effect a synthesis. With this the picture of the *Human Being as Music* arises. A description of eurythmy gestures will not be given, but rather an attempt is made to bring experiences into a harmony. In the Appendix the sources are listed and the most important statements of Steiner are quoted. Yet his explanations should be read in context, for only then does a living picture arise of the abundance of his spiritual gifts. Compared with speech eurythmy, little has been published on music eurythmy. After the music eurythmy course of 1924, which Steiner had wanted to follow with further courses, his death in 1925 left many questions and problems open which could no longer be answered by him. Thus we have had the responsibility for our own work and study and must find our own path.

These observations have arisen from the awareness of some difficulties in the domain of music eurythmy and music. They are meant primarily for eurythmists, but also for musicians and all those who are looking to the image of the human being in anthroposophy for a stimulus for the experience of music.

Introduction

The human being reveals his own being in the world through his artistic creations. Rudolf Steiner showed, for each art, from what aspects of human nature the artist draws the impulses and the forces which he can realize in his work. In the circle of arts — architecture, sculpture, painting, music, poetry/drama, eurythmy — he placed music in the middle. The musician takes the power for musical creation from his ego, in which as a seed for the future the impulses of the Spirit-self are active, and sends these laws inherent in the ego down into his astral body. (i) [1]

Music thus appears on the threshold between the *future* spiritual part of the human being and those parts already created. It is the means by which the ego carries the spiritual forces which come towards it, into the earthly world. But this is only achieved as far as this earthly world is within the human being, namely, into the astral body. This 'starry body' of man is the composite radiating of the whole starry cosmos which the human being has passed through on his descent into birth. Through the incoming ego, the inner starry organism increasingly becomes an instrument upon which the unconscious cosmic recollections resound as musical laws; music resounds as a completely human creation.

The 'visual arts', architecture, sculpture and painting, which appear as creations in the visible world, in space, were brought by Steiner to a culminating collaboration in the miraculous building of the First Goetheanum. The 'sounding' arts, music and poetry (the latter only coming to resound through the art of recitation and declamation) he complemented with the newly created 'youngest art', *eurythmy*. This brings to visible form in space as 'visible speech' and 'visible singing' the movements that otherwise only sound invisibly in the flow of time of speech and music. The visible collaboration of the 'spatial arts' in the First Goetheanum came about through their metamorphosis, which brought them into motion so that the flowing laws of time and development came to expression. The building was a 'house of the Word'. Its resting forms enclosed speech and the gestures of movement as a shell does its kernel. Here the future goal which Steiner had indicated for the visual arts was realized, that sculptural and architectural form should 'become musical'. [2]

To speak or to write about music easily leads into the danger of remaining stuck in concepts. This would completely lead away from the musical element, where everything is still intensive 'experience', soul activity and movement. Real musical experience is related to dreaming. 'The artist must be able to dream, or dream whilst being awake, that is: he must be able to meditate.' You have to pay attention, not to any specific content, but only to soul tensions and resolutions, 'like the action of a dream; then is the dream indeed a thing of music'. This intensive, inwardly experienced movement is the actual 'content' of music. [3]

As Goethe expresses it:

> The majesty of art appears perhaps most preeminently with music, because it has no material that has to be considered. It is entirely form and content, raising and enobling everything that it expresses. [4]

And Steiner:

> In truth the melodic element is the content of music ... this unconscious element that rules in the dream, that rules in the musical element, precisely as the melodic element ... *melos* (ii) is the musical element. From this you see that the musical element has a content, not the thematic content which is taken from the sensory world, but rather that particular content which actually appears clearly wherever something is expressed in the sense world, but in such a way that what relates to the senses can be left out, so that you then have the actual essence of the thing. The actual musical element, the spiritual in music, is between the notes, lies in the intervals, (iii) is that which you do not hear. [3]

On our journey into the realm of music we will be led into the realm of the inaudible. It is a path of experience, analogous to the path of initiation. Thus experience of music can become a path of training which leads to higher levels of knowledge.

A *first* step leads us to active *differentiated perception* of otherwise closely connected musical elements.

The *second* step demands that we inwardly enliven the individual elements we experience, to grasp as creative forces their soul-qualities through the polarities effective in them. To lay hold of our experience we call upon the image-creating forces of the soul, we create *Imaginations*. (i)

On the *third* stage we seek between the polarities, which necessitates our finding a way out through our own free activity. We open up the image forms, and move in the realm of the inaudible towards what resounds from the future. With prophetic forces we grasp and form what does not yet have existence. We practise striving towards *Inspiration*.

On the *fourth* stage we must learn to guide and focus our consciousness in conformity with that which is to be formed. We must have the courage to lose ourselves in order then to take hold of ourselves once again from outside. We must be able to experience ourselves within the whole of a musical event, even before we witness the individual details in the flow of time. This corresponds to the creative *'anticipation'* of the artist. This is the preparatory schooling for the experience of *Intuition*.

Practice in this way, by means of artistic activity, is made possible by the precise indications for music eurythmy. The greatest stimulation for an extending and deepening of musical experience can proceed from it.

REFERENCES

(i) Imagination, Inspiration, and Intuition are technical terms. See Steiner, *An Outline of Occult Science* (Chapter 5) AP New York, RSP London (GA13), for clarification on all points of terminology (Translators' note).

(ii) Melos (Gk for 'tune') is the inner power that forms melodies, not the finished melody which, of course, includes rhythm and beat (Translators' note).

(iii) In the present book, the term 'interval' primarily refers to a pitch interval, that is, a melodic interval. The degrees of the scale also function as 'intervals' (see p. 29). A third function, that of harmony ('vertical' interval), shows that eurythmy often involves possibilities which can be summarized as 'not only, but also' (Translators' note).

Cosmic Music

'In the beginning was the Logos.' Everything came into being out of the Logos. We could say 'cosmic Word' or 'cosmic Sound' instead. In the beginning it was a unity expressed in a twofold revelation. The human being was created in the image of the Godhead, as a representation of the universe, as 'microcosmos'. [5] He was created out of 'cosmic Music', as the 'true' human being, without yet having to be subject to the laws of incarnation. He was placed on the earth. He became subject to the laws of corporeality. He was, however, endowed with speech, and through this he became a bearer of higher hierarchic powers of intelligence.

In this division between body and spirit, the soul yearns unconsciously for its lost homeland in the spirit-realm. When it is released from the body during sleep it rises up through the spheres to the spiritual world where it has its original home. Thence it brings with it into waking consciousness primeval forces which are not of an earthly nature. The human being experiences these forces in the earthly realm as *music*.

When we listen to music we are reminded in the very depths of our soul of our spiritual homeland. Thence comes the enlivening, healing effect of music. In music we experience a recollection of our primeval cosmic form. [6] The primeval human being appears as the *being 'Music'*.

Music lives in time. But it is not tied to the measure of time. In our concept of 'time' the actual stream of life, the etheric stream of time, has been lost. This stream can only be revealed in measures of time, in rhythms, but as *creating principle* it contain stillness and movement, quickness and slowness, future and past, and creates in the streams of 'forwards' and 'backwards' an actual 'time-space', which makes it possible to imagine beforehand and to recollect.

When music becomes audible it carries this *being of time* into the realm of *space*. It stirs up the world of space, brings it into vibrating motion, acting creatively or destructively. It impresses the forming forces of the sound-ether into the substance of the physical world. The results of its activity appear in the formations of the plant and mineral kingdoms. [7]

When music sounds, we experience the penetration of another sphere into our everyday world. That is why it is tragic when 'music' is degraded to the production of noise. Only regular vibration produces musical sound. The laws of the starry realms are active in it. For this reason we recognise a kinship of music to astronomy and mathematics. But just as we must learn to grasp the element of *'time'* as the creative *stream of life*, so should we free *'music'* from the calculative concepts of mathematical acoustics. What is more, we must learn to see in the numerical relationships of the vibrations of the notes more than only the division of the vibrating string. All these things are only the means whereby music can make its 'appearance' in our sensory realm. We 'take hold' of music, however, somewhere else quite different from the ear which perceives the sound. The ear is 'actually there to overcome the sounding of the note in the air and to cast the pure etheric experience of the note back into our inner being'. [8]

Music is a sovereign, creative being. It lives in the 'proportions, the tensions'; that means, in the *movements* of 'entities'. Steiner said that the 'music of the spheres' of the ancient Greeks was experienced in the reciprocal *proportions* of the *movements* of the *heavenly bodies*, in other words, in the infinitely differentiated interplay, the continuously changing relationships in the cosmos, within which the human being experiences himself to be standing. This is portrayed in the human being, in the subtle movements of our rhythmic nature, the natural play of breathing and heartbeat in connection with the life-processes of our internal organs, supported by the miraculous structure of our bones. [9]

The Human Being and Music

If the human being, as enlivened, ensouled, spirit-bearing form, is created out of cosmic music, then in turn it is the *human being* alone who can produce music here on the earth. For no sound of an animal, no sound of a natural thing, is really *music*. Only human beings can *sing*, only they can build *instruments* and make them sound, only they can make their own *human frame* to 'sing' in music eurythmy, in *'visible singing'*. They are indeed revealed as human beings in every movement of music eurythmy, for this is *'solely human'*. 'For the musical element is not akin to nature, but solely human'. [10]

What causes someone to produce sounds? No sound arises in a person unless their soul wishes to free itself from the experience of joy or sorrow. In a state of being profoundly moved it seeks a way out of the excess, it 'expresses' itself in sound. [11] That is one reason for the existence of music: its sounds arise from the depths of the human soul.

However, there is a second way to reach music: when someone discovers how the objects in the world contain hidden 'sounds' which in turn only he, the human being, can release. If we strike stacked, stripped tree trunks we hear distinct sounds. When we strike clay, glass or metal vessels, the sounds they make are clear and differentiated. This does not apply, however, to a living tree or a lump of metal. We must first fashion this material to enable it to resound. Likewise the pan-pipes and the taut string. And *what* we cause to resound from them is once again our relationship with the world of joy and sorrow. Today *in the way we deal with music intellectually* we are far removed from the actual essence of music which is in reality man's most intimate concern, for it arises out of him, and his relationship to the world is reflected in its laws.

Music as 'Human Being'

If the connection of 'Human Being: Music' is so significant and exact, then all the laws and elements of music must be discoverable in the human being, and conversely the aspects of man's being and the possibilities of human consciousness must present themselves in music. From Steiner's indications and suggestions for *music eurythmy* much can be developed with practice that can lead to an idea of what 'the Human Being as Music' might be.

Steiner described the process of perceiving music [8] on the basis of the rhythmical interplay of breathing and the movement of the cerebral fluid, which in its effects is continued in the circulating blood. This conjures up before the inner eye an extraordinary human form as an organ, as an 'instrument' for experiencing music. It closely resembles those very first representations of man which we know as 'idols' from what is called the Cycladic culture, those statues, mostly flat, sculptured out of stone outlining the human form, the simplest of which is more like a violin than a human being; a 'torso' surrounded by a Cassinian curve, with a long narrow 'neck' pushing upwards. No head, no limbs. A violin strongly resembles this figure. The violin, however, has strings stretched across it, the instrument itself is but a resonating body. The strings are caused to vibrate by the gliding bow drawn by the musician's arm. Steiner tells us, [12] that *instruments* are *Imaginations* created and formed out of matter by the human being. In the violin family and similar instruments we have thus an Imagination of the middle, the torso of the human being and also of the human embryo at a particular stage in its development, when it lives (apart from the head that already exists) in this limbless form. And then 'the limbs shoot on to it' — the cosmos as it were rays them from outside towards it and it takes hold of them, incorporating them into its form. [13]

When the arms are used in the movements of music eurythmy, they are really like a kind of membrane that enables people to transfer the vibrations of the world of music into the rest of their organism so that this moves in accordance with the music, it 'sings'; they are, as it were, the bow which causes the strings of the violin to resound. But the 'player' of this instrument, the actual 'singer', feels himself as the centre; he acts from the middle, from the rhythmic system outwards into all the possibilities of musically attuned movement. He learns thus to identify his 'Music as Human Being' more and more with the 'Human Being as Music'.

'The Human Being as Music'

She was called 'Musica' in the Middle Ages; she was represented in Renaissance painting in the round dance of the seven liberal arts as a lovely female figure; Music as a being in human form. Let us question her about the aspects of her being through which she appears to us and influences us.

What moves us initially, quite spontaneously, in the experience of listening is surely melody, or more exactly, the rise and fall of *melos*, the sequence of notes. Here the soul experiences itself directly in movement, it rises up into light-filled levity or sinks downwards into the dark depths of its own hidden inwardness. It experiences the objective realities of joy and sorrow, of brightness and darkness of soul. It grasps what it means to approach the light of the spirit or to become aware of the might of the emotions while imprisoned in the body. Steiner termed these extremes of experience *ethos* and *pathos*.

This *melos* experience, however, does not remain by itself. We notice how it articulates itself, differentiates, tarries here, rushes forward there. Through the rapid sequence of notes we are stimulated, wanting ourselves to join in with the movement, hastening from note to note, running to meet the goal; we feel excited, awakened, filled by the impressions sounding in on us. [14] With long, sustained notes, on the contrary, we feel as if held fast; the long note fills us with monotony, takes possession of us while we feel ourselves being extinguished, pushed out of our soul-spaces; we feel ourselves becoming empty; it is akin to the process of falling asleep.

When both these experiences come to us alternately we feel it like a rhythmically articulated process of breathing: filling up – emptying out; inhaling – exhaling; waking up – falling asleep. And we experience the invigoration of such an 'alternation of breathing'. We are within the vital element of *rhythm*.

When *melos* and rhythm combine in our experience we are already quite close to the phenomenon of music itself, because the one makes use of the other for differentiated formation. Musical structure only receives a really contoured form, however, when a third element is added which in our experience is felt more unconsciously, but which we somehow miss when it is absent. This element is like the bed of the river over which the stream of water flows, which limits, constrains, gives direction, regulates the gradient – *beat*.

Historically, beat is the youngest member of the 'body' of music, appearing only in the fifteenth to seventeenth centuries. Through it music can really incarnate. It arranges itself into accented and unaccented elements. The connection to earthly heaviness is dealt with in different ways. The 'march' in the true sense becomes possible (who can resist a well-played march?) and so does the 'waltz'.

In the co-ordination of these three elements *melos, rhythm,* and *beat* a structure becomes possible which produces the actual manifestation of music in our age: the *phrase.* The phrase, or motif, is the tangible expression in music corresponding to the *word* which embodies the being 'speech'. Speech and music are inexhaustible, like the cosmos. In the *word* and in the phrase they appear incarnated, individualized, each as a self-sufficient organism, having its own character, a personal face, expressing something. That is why unlimited possibilities can exist. But without 'phrases' music can express nothing essential. We should not say that 'music built in phrases' is old-fashioned and has been superseded. The phrase has but changed its mode of appearance in contemporary music. Whether it appears as 'row', as 'series', as 'sequence' or otherwise, no music is composed without some such 'rule' or structure. Steiner called the three elements of movement: *melos,* rhythm and beat. In each of these 'the inner, actual life of the phrase' is working in a finely differentiated experience of tension between two poles.

We can really lay hold of something of the mobile nature of the garments, the *envelopes* of the being of music in the three elements which have real connections to the enveloping organism, the 'bodies' of the human being. In *melos* we feel the sentient body of music, in rhythm the life-body, and in beat, music finally reaches that structure and support which corresponds to the physical body (this, it is true, is the oldest of the human envelopes but only on the earth does it become filled with material and falls prey to gravity, just as beat appears as the final and most external musical element).

If we begin to listen more sensitively, we can witness something of how the soul aspects develop out of the bodily envelopes. In the streaming of *melos* upwards and downwards the soul begins to feel how 'up' means light for the soul, striving upwards gives it joy; how 'down' is darkness, but also warmth, the downward climb can be sorrow, struggle, and resistance, but strength too; these are experiences of the *sentient soul* in the *heights* and *depths* of *pitch.*

The contrasting ways of experiencing the *intellectual* or *mind soul* are heard in the weaving *rhythm,* of the etheric body of music, where the soul discovers how it lives in continuous interchange with its surroundings in the differentiated *duration of notes* sometimes in a lively manner, sometimes as if falling asleep, filled and empty.

In strictly structured *beat,* which performs the function of dividing time into measurable and comparable units, thus giving music the structure through which it can literally *step out* into the world - in this physical element of tempo, weight is effective in strict regularity. This unyielding figure governs the heavy and light part of the bar. But when the *will*, which has up to now gone along in time as though asleep, begins to wake up and takes the division of stress into its own hand, handling its influence on the sound with a certain will of its own, then the sovereign accent appears, loud and soft, *forte* and *piano*: the forces of the *consciousness soul* begin to be effective.

Necessity and Freedom

Up to this point everything is bound by necessity and subject to the effect of polarities. But the soul strives to free itself from the compulsion of opposites, by creating a space where it can be freely active and creative. It has to be creative in order not to lose itself, it must give rein to the 'play drive', and it is not for nothing that making music is called 'playing'. [15] Players, interpreters that is, and also eurythmists, have to capture creative freedom whatever the laws that bind them. They do this within the three elements of music, in three *inaudible*, but all the more effective, activities. Through them we truly enter into the being of music, which, in reality, lives in the realm of the inaudible. [16]

Beat is effective, controlling time, dividing it up. There seems to be no way out. But we *use* our freedom when a bar of music has run its course by setting a boundary to the beat: we draw a line, the *bar line* in fact. It takes up no time and yet it concludes a certain period in time. In this timeless moment we withdraw from the unyielding mechanical progression of time measures and our return into 'time' is an act of freedom, an independent step which could equally well not happen if we so chose. And this gives the new first beat of the next bar its new energy to begin afresh. It is like an immeasurably short sleep out of which we awaken strengthened every time. Our consciousness knocks into this 'border post' bar line as though against an obstacle overcome, and we proceed with secure steps forwards into the new bar, into the future (and never into the past). [N.B. 'Bar' = American 'measure', 'bar line' = American 'bar'.]

Rhythm arises through the longer or shorter duration of notes. These lay hold of the flow of time, forming and shaping it according to their various lengths. They fill our soul, holding it fast by their sound. If a note is long, then it holds us for a long time under its spell. If we experience a progression of short notes, then a rapid movement appears possible. The movement, however, is only a step from one note to another, and it is always brought to a standstill by the new note. Its form of duration, even if it is short, clothes us and forces us to tarry. Only when we can escape the play of this pattern, when we can bring the sounding to silence, can we experience the actual stream of life, music's effective power of movement, and that is the *rest*. We could say: the note is form in time. The longer the note, the less the movement, the shorter the note the greater the movement, and when the note disappears completely then *movement* alone governs. And this movement is the manifestation of the living element in time. And if we could experience (like Faust) the 'universe' in this inaudible 'nothing', if it is a 'creative rest', then we return revitalized into the sounding weaving of the musical passage, delighting in creating.

The stream of *melos* carries the feeling soul up with it into the utmost heights of heaven and pulls it down into the deepest abysses of hell; the soul can experience and feel itself tossed to and fro by unfathomable fate, torn between angels and devils, between ideal and disaster, so long as it swims in this stream drawn along without seeing a beginning or an end, without being able to grasp an aim. But if we succeed in stopping this apparently senseless being-dragged-along and in canalizing this apparently endless stream, in running off single streams from the whole, forming them, and determining their beginning and end, then they begin to become meaningful statements. And as the singer, through taking in breath, shapes and interprets meaningfully the phrases of a song, and as every musician through phrasing forms the *melos* element into melody, into the specific *phrase*, so the soul can feel how it progressively becomes the master and the shaper of its experiences. It learns to conclude an experience or a thought, to free itself from it, to rise above it for a fresh beginning. To turn from chaos into a meaningful, ordered cosmos, to set itself goals and also to grasp them with certainty, that is the power which the soul learns to wield when it learns to fashion consciously in the stream of notes and to fly courageously over yawning gaps. The breath between the phrases, the *Motiv-Schwung*, a movement which again occurs outside time, in order then to grasp the new beginning within time, is the third inaudible creative element.

Centre and Periphery

That which exists (The Note)

True music has to be sought in the realm of the inaudible. But in order to appear in our earthly world it cannot but enter into what can be heard. For after all, our musical experience is stimulated by what we 'hear'. We could have no earthly music if there were no *notes*.

'Heavenly music', the music of the spheres, occurs in relationships of movements in pure spiritual activity. Here on earth there only exist relationships of something to something else; movement arises from the tension between polarities. Activity is directed towards a goal.

A string can resound only when it is held at both ends, that is, when it is taut and set into motion. Then it transmits its vibrations to the air and we hear a note. This has led to the misunderstanding that the oscillating air is the note. It is, however, only the 'vehicle' which the note has to make use of to reach us.

Yet once the note is there; is it 'the music'? As little as the temple in all its architectural beauty is the Godhead who is to dwell in it, just as little is the note the music. But it builds the 'dwelling' in which the goddess music can live. We enter between the pillars of the notes and these are the portals through which we enter the inner sanctuary, that mysterious 'space' of music, constantly self-creating, alone decreeing its own laws, and in these laws, to our awed astonishment, we rediscover the human being. So long as we move in the realm of the external enveloping aspects, we still remain subject to the laws of the earthly world, we experience directions which correspond to the external organization of space. *Melos* leads us upwards and downwards. Rhythm lets us move forwards or attaches us firmly to the realm 'behind us'. Beat strides with its measured walk alternating between right and left. These are the dimensions of space in which we find ourselves bodily placed, and in which our soul moves in diverse ways as well.

If we wish to enter the 'inner sanctuary', however, we have to leave the world of three dimensions behind. If a spatial image helps, then it could be that of a globe, the spherical expanse in whose centre we find ourselves, whose periphery is formed for us by the stars.

If we feel ourselves from an earthly standpoint in the centre of this tremendous circle of stars, and 'enter into' the raying out of a particular star which reaches us, then something comes into being much like the string of an instrument, one end of which rests with us while the other remains with the star. Through our musical intention we cause it to vibrate, and hence to resound.

We can place our human form, which conforms with primeval cosmic proportions, into these 'directing rays' of the cosmos and if we 'go out to meet' them we become an instrument upon which the stars can cause their specific relationships, their vibrations, to resound. When we stretch our arms (those limbs joined onto us from the cosmos, from the periphery) out to the stars, we make ourselves into an image of cosmic proportions. This raying figure of inexhaustible possibilities of connection to the periphery of the cosmos can indeed become a 'presentation' of the sounding universe. We know that the open string of an instrument can resound sympathetically when the corresponding note sounds nearby; we no longer find it astonishing when a small electric apparatus with the help of a little length of wire can catch music out of the empty air. Should the miraculous construction of our skeleton be a worse instrument? But it would all depend upon bringing it into the completely exact 'tuning'.

Now the number of notes offered us by the universe is inexhaustible. We have to choose. Already our ear itself limits us to a relatively small extract from the middle of the whole tonal range. Yet we know that other earthly inhabitants can perceive notes of higher and lower frequencies than we can. From the ever abundant fullness of notes available to us, we have to find *those* which 'apply' to us as human beings, which in their relationships to one another and to us present a living reality, in which we rediscover our human nature.

As we have chosen out of the rich spectrum of colours the seven main colours which we can see in the rainbow, as we recognize from ancient wisdom among all the moving heavenly bodies the number seven as belonging to the evolution of mankind and of the earth, so are we disposed to accept the scale of seven main notes as the one suitable for us.

This has not always been so. Humanity in more ancient epochs 'heard' in much more widely-spaced intervals, thus hearing different notes from those we hear today. [17] Not so very long ago (and in other parts of the earth, this is still the same today) people used the five-note scale. The structure of the scale has changed continuously. The single note has for a while now no longer been what it was even a few centuries ago, through tempering and through the heightening of the tuning. Our notes like our scale have become conventional. No wonder that endeavours to break through this convention appear, either by using 1/3 or 1/4 tones, or to extend the scale to 12 notes and thus to arrive at an image of the zodiac.

Steiner found it important for whatever concerns the *human being* to establish the relation of the concept of *twelve* to the concept of *seven*. [18] The human being in his sevenfold nature reflects the sevenfold influences of the planets. All the rhythms of his development on the earth run in periods of seven, even though the twelvefold cosmos (represented by the zodiac) also lies behind them. Thus the scale of seven notes became the truly human scale of our time. Human evolution is expressed in it. Although in the twelvefold circle of the stars the formative forces of space define the human form, yet the stirring impulses of the seven planets are effective in the rhythmic life-processes, which form the enveloping aspects for the life of the soul, which follows threefold laws. Thus the sevenfold rhythm of life is a manifestation of reality that accords with man.

In our classical and romantic music we also employ semitones as a matter of course — where would we be without chromaticism? Polyphony and modulation would not be possible. And after all, we do find the whole chromatic sequence contained in the overtone series. Modern development leads to a very free dealing in the realm of notes, pressing on for ever finer division and differentiation. [19]

Steiner indicated something else: to come to a differentiation through penetration into the single note, to discover in the single note a melody consisting of at least three notes; how the note sounding in the present calls forth melodically both recollection and expectancy as adjacent notes. [20] This can lead us to find in the note itself an element of development, a force of movement, which leads it over from mere proportions of space into a life in time.

That which is active (The Interval)

If in the realm of notes we see a reflection of the resounding universe, an echo of that cosmic Logos which created and formed the universe, then we are in a situation where our personal experience breaks down. Our feeling is silenced when the Godhead speaks. We take refuge in the image and live in that.

However, when we discover that between the majestic resounding pillars of the building of the universe gates open up, doors are flung wide, through which we, with our feeling and active humanity are able to enter, then we can arrive at the most inward part of resounding space. Here we cannot help being active. And our activity puts us into ever new, ever different relationships with our surroundings. We change ourselves from step to step, from degree to degree; the stream of development passes right through us. What we do will form the world and at the same time it works back on ourselves. Here we lose all conceptions of forwards and backwards, of great and small, of earlier and later in their normal meaning. Only the movement from inside to outside, or from outside to inside, only the gesture of giving and receiving retains its validity; it becomes infinitely differentiated.

Here in the realm of *intervals* we have reached the creative centre of the divine being of music; with this being we have to identify ourselves. We have to allow the creative powers of our ego to work in our soul; then they can pour into our form and come to expression through movement and gesture. Once again, as when we lay hold of the notes, it is our limbs which supply the instrument, but now in a wonderful, pre-formed differentiation. And this time our activity proceeds from the centre, and sends out willing and feeling, the whole stream of movement out into the miraculous form of our arms, which in fact, according to how they are taken hold of, are translated into movement to give it out into the surrounding space.

The bony structure of our arms is a wonderful instrument, and so is that of our legs in a somewhat different form. And although each individual interval corresponds to a specific bone formation, the movement does not necessarily need to happen proportionately in space. Thus, for example, a 'large' interval can be formed much smaller than a 'small' one. It depends solely on the intensity of the soul experience which creates an expression for itself.

Here 'large' and 'small', 'inner' and 'outer' are created completely afresh, and a new 'dimension' arises which is formed out of the soul intensities alone. Whether the sounds are of 'longer' or 'shorter' duration, 'higher' or 'lower' in pitch, they play only a subsidiary role.

We were already obliged in the realm of the enveloping aspect to seek a free activity working in the inaudible realm, in order to penetrate to the truly musical essence, and this gave us an inkling, as a preparatory stage for what occurs here when we work with the powers of the intervals.

For the ear which registers external sound, the interval is silent. It is indistinguishable from a rest, and for the ear this is an emptiness. But for the experiencing soul, it can contain a tremendous richness of experience. It demands courage to leave the haven of the audible, to push off from the note, and with active anticipation of the future to traverse the 'valley between', until on the farther shore a new note quiets the stimulated soul, receiving the creative movement, bringing it to rest.

It really is an 'adventure of the soul' to plunge yourself as though into the 'nothing', to fashion the future in anticipation, to experience it completely, long before it steps into existence. But also the note, into which this streaming power of the soul merges, is taken hold of and transformed.

We can experience and fashion an interval from any note to any note. Then we live in the progressing melody.

We can also fashion intervals measured from a constant key-note to the other notes of the scale. Then after a while the notes of the scale become identified with the activity of the intervals through which we reach them. Then this activity wraps itself like a quality around the note, which becomes a *'degree of the scale'*. Thus the note 'G' in the scale of C major can appear as the 5th degree with the quality of the fifth. In D major it would be clothed with the fourth and show itself as the 4th degree; in G major it would be the key-note itself. The single note can thus carry out in the whole transformation space of music the most variable 'functions' by being penetrated by the power of the intervals.

When we are able to form the *degrees of the scale* and the melodic *interval* differently in eurythmic movements, we have a rich abundance of expressive possibilities.

To the expressive gestures for the perception of individual intervals, Steiner added the *forms* (choreography) which are executed in space. [12] These show a clear relationship with the form of the images we know as *Chladni's sound figures* which show clearly the form-generating power of the vibrating sounds.

In the eurythmic fashioning we can thus allow the soul-experience, the living, fully creative movement and the forming power of the intervals to become visible simultaneously.

With this activity, although it appears in visible space, we are nevertheless free from the laws of space. But we can voluntarily enter into the laws of the other musical elements. When we live in *melody* with our activity of creating intervals, we follow the ascent happily, without any trouble; we could, however, be required to follow its descent too, and here the task becomes more complex for we have to turn our experience to a completely different situation. An expansive interval released in an ascending series of notes is easily fashioned in the 'more rarefied air', so to speak, of the higher registers. But if, let us say, we have to fashion a descending sixth or seventh, we enter the more concentrated sphere of the deeper registers bound to the body, and the contradiction of the intervallic will with the quality of direction in which it is to be led has a clear effect. The energy of the interval, which of necessity is strengthened, struggles against the condensing gravity; something comes into being which is comparable to the experience of an explosion. The difference is not so drastically felt with the smaller intervallic steps and yet there is a big difference whether an activity, according to my feeling, turns towards the vicinity of clear mental images or whether it sinks inwards and unites with the will in the more muffled depths of the soul. The effect is like the substances of an aggregate as they solidify or dissolve.

When we combine our forming of intervals with the element of *rhythm* this is above all expressed in the way it is presented in space. If we have a lot of time in the realm of long notes to shape the movement, it will appear clearly in its sculptural strength (this particularly affects the choreography), indeed it will even strive to penetrate into the temporal realm of the notes. The quality-forming effect of the formation of the degree of the scale becomes more essential; the image element checking movement becomes stronger. If, however, we get caught in the strong current of rapidly succeeding notes, we have little time to present our gestures; we have to enter quickly into the activity of shaping them, for the forms of movement crystalize as quick as lightning at the moment of contact and dissolve again, like snowflakes, to make way for the next shaped figuration.

In the quick-light, in the slow-dark stream of time we live with our activity. Is it so transient, so without efficacy, as it might appear? A great mystery is linked to this organism of time: just as consciousness of the interval creates a necessity to anticipate the future (and it has the power to do so, too), so it can also experience the transition into duration, of what happens in time. What arises as shaping form from our activity, what in the next moment appears to belong to the past, remains, because it is caught by consolidating time behind us, stands so to speak in image-like form around us in the spaces condensed out of time, and creates the background against which the further events can meaningfully take place. Thus we come now to experience for the first time the *whole* of a musical event. [21]

All the intervallic formations discussed up to now proceeded from us, from the active, moving human being. We always knew: I am the point of depature, I am myself the fundamental note (whether according to the key or for each fresh interval), I move towards the note that I want to reach. But when it arises that from a note recognized by me in its intervallic quality, the movement streams back to the fundamental, streams, that is, to me, then this cannot be just a normal descending interval. A completely different activity of consciousness becomes necessary. First I have to transfer my consciousness into the character of that other note, and then with my own centre of activity, my own 'fundamental' or 'key-note', *go to where the other is*, that is *identify* myself with it. Then I experience the working of the other in myself. The indication which Steiner gave about this exercise sounds easy. Its realization depends upon a complete about turn of consciousness. It is like a preliminary exercise for what we term 'Intuition'. [22]

In some activities of music eurythmy we experience something like images of quite particular conditions or events of soul and spirit. We experience an intervallic movement as an activity coming from normal earthly consciousness. But in the movement for the interval falling back to the key-note we can find an image for that condition of consciousness of the soul after death, in which it has to identify everything it has done here on the earth and live through the effects in its own being. [23]

The Realm of the Heart: Major and Minor

The source of all musical activity lies in the heart realm of the being of music. Here, in the great heartbeat, the primal movement of all life resounds, the systole and diastole, the contracting and expanding which is shown archetypally in every breath. For life is not manifested in unity. Its heartbeat arises from duality, *polarity*. Light and dark, spirit and matter, expansion and contraction, dying and being born stand opposite each other, mutually interpenetrating in growth and decay, in joy and sorrow, health and illness, and yet remain polar opposites like sun and moon. In music they are termed: *major* and *minor*.

With this, however, we do not mean only what we normally describe as the major or minor triad in classical harmony, as the harmonic element or types of notes. We should not say that for contemporary music it has been irrelevant ιow for a long time. What we describe as major and minor is much more the basic direction, the way it works, the dominating character which is necessary for every musical statement, indeed for every human expression. After all, even our most modern contemporaries have to breathe, and the only way their hearts can beat is in systole and diastole.

The human being produces notes from no other source than out of pleasure or pain. Either one feels drawn out of oneself in experiencing pleasure and sends the note after the soul, streaming out in order to halt it — it is notes in the major which sound outwards — or one feels oneself compressed by pain and searches to give the tormented soul a way out: it is notes in the minor which break forth from the suffering, seeking to release the pressure. [11]

In these moments of genesis the gesture, direction and character are already given. Steiner's descriptions of the characters of the major and the minor are very pictorial and clear. Health and illness stand opposite each other, laughing and weeping, doing and being done to. Proceeding out of yourself in every form is a manifestation of the major, turning in on yourself, a manifestation of the minor.

Both opposing motions, however, imply each other; neither can exist without the other. The ancient sign of the involuting and evolving spiral, which appears among all peoples at the beginning of their culture, expresses this basic truth: 'Behold thyself, behold the world'. And the ancient challenge, 'know thyself', can only be fulfilled through the completion: 'know the world'. Inhalation demands exhalation, waking needs sleeping as its completion, summer needs winter, death needs life. [24]

When we listen more deeply we notice how the one always works effectively within the other, how the external and the internal always mutually correspond. In inhalation, which is a motion streaming inwards, the lungs expand; in exhalation, which we experience as expanding motion, the lungs contract. Being born is the beginning of a process of death, death is birth in the spirit. Shell and kernel, fruit and seed, body and spirit are such contrasting, interdependent opposites. In the metamorphosis from the one to the other, the soul's breathing is at work, which we could call the source of 'major' and 'minor'.

> Die Welt im Ich erbauen,
> Das Ich in Welten schauen
> Ist Seelenatem ... [24]

> To build the world in the 'I'
> To behold the 'I' in the world
> Is breathing of the soul ...

The major mood arises in the working together of the aspects of the human being whenever a higher principle 'outsounds' a lower one. If the lower principle rules over the higher, the instrument is tuned to 'minor'. [25] Minor is the feeling of being bound within oneself, fastened to the body, perceiving oneself more strongly (right up to the experience of pain). This can, however, call forth a certain enjoyment, a defiant feeling of strength; but also an opening up of oneself in order to receive something else within, a being-filled, a receiving. If we look for a correspondence in the domain of speech it is to be found in the vowels A and E (är and ā) which bring a similar experience to expression. Both nuances of the minor, the receiving and the closing within oneself are clearly formed in the gestures. And in the expressive gesture for 'minor' both are present too: the direction from without inwards, the being-filled and perceiving oneself, indeed even that self-assertive warding off of an all-too-strong pressure. There are consequently almost opposite possibilities of movement.

We feel the major as a streaming out, as a freeing of ourselves from corporeal bondage, as the element of will which urges us outwards to deeds; we emanate joy and strength, growing beyond ourselves until we almost lose ourselves. Here too, however, interest for an 'other' can arise; we strive towards it, wishing to unite with it, to become 'one' with it. In the vowels U and O (ōō and ō) we find the corresponding sounds, the streaming out from ourselves and the finding ourselves in 'the other'. Thus the gesture for 'major' also contains both possibilities: a streaming out, expanding of ourselves and a confident urging forwards, a giving ourselves a hold outside ourselves. In A – E and O – U the human relationship to the world is expressed in sound by minor and major.

What is the 'I' (ē)? Here the human being experiences himself. Where is it in music? Between the major experience and the minor experience a balance can arise 'in the transition', a suspended moment of 'neither-nor', or of the linking 'and'. It cannot be held fast, it has always to be created afresh, similar to the rest, to the breath (*Motiv-Schwung*), indeed even similar to the bar-line where we have to create the situation of balance 'out of nothing', as it were. It is a moment of freedom, as if we were to feel ourselves standing upright on the earth, freed for a split second from being bound to sun and moon, and then out of a free resolve to proceed further on our path of destiny.

The human heartbeat, too, does not run on as mechanically as a machine. Between one heartbeat and the next there lies an unnoticeable caesura, as though life holds its breath for a timeless moment. Here life is placed into our hands — thank goodness, however, into the hands of our higher being.

If we are able so to fashion the major and minor influences through the 'I (ē) experience' that balance is preserved, then we are able to deal with it 'harmoniously'. If, however, it falls out of our control, if it is mixed in an arbitrary way, making a chaotic, confused effect, then it becomes discordant. This comes to expression in a eurythmic gesture which presents the opposite of the 'I (ē)'. Compelled to follow major and minor *simultaneously*, we have to make two contrary steps at the same time: a jump is the result which, through the bending of the knee associated with it, drags our whole form downwards; we are so to speak 'thrown down to the earth', falling into chaos.

We can only release ourselves by 'erasing' what has been, as though it had not happened. This demands the strength of decision and activity. If we are able to erase the chaos generated, we can aspire again to the state of balance, and from this freshly gained 'I (ē)' situation we can place ourselves anew and freely into existence. In every cadence which closes every musical experience in classical music our soul is reminded slightly of this image of the cosmic process of humanity which we call the 'fall of man' and together with our striving to overcome it. In the chord sequence I IV V I, where V is the dominant seventh chord, there is contained the memory and the reminder of our earthly situation.

If this cadence takes effect as a law of arrangement in space, it demonstrates its fashioning, synthesizing strength. The musical occurrence can 'occupy' in a suitable way the articulated space, can flow through it, and can thus appear in its transformations in space.

It is certainly symptomatic that in our time discordant harmonies in music dominate. Pure major or minor are hardly employed. Music is striving away from the triads, indeed from tonality in general.

But the *qualities* of major and minor are found as characteristics in all music. They obtain in the releasing or binding character of music, in the rising or falling course of tonal progressions, in the intervals proceeding outwards or inwards. In the fashioning of themes, too, in the sequence of musical statements we can feel the streaming in or streaming out, the oppressing or the releasing. Only, faced with music that is 'merely constructed', when we are no longer able to feel, does the experience of this human-cosmic breathing cease.

The Threefold 'Human Being as Music'

The heart is an organ of perception. [26] Its faculty of perception is feeling. This is an objective force of the soul, which can be guided, adjusted and developed (like hearing, seeing, touching). In the musical realm we can neither perceive nor act without feeling. The homeland of feeling is the heart region; from there it can stream into all the other areas of the human being, changing them, changing itself. [27]

When feeling streams from its own realm, the human centre, the *rhythmic system*, upwards towards the *head*, it approaches the place where thinking rules. If feeling is to remain within the musical realm, it must not be allowed to reach that realm of the head system where *thinking* is effective. For there it would be grasped by the brilliance of the thought world and transformed into concepts, into ideas. Ideas and concepts, however, are extra-musical forces which would transform music into speech. [28]

When musical feeling is poured downwards into the *system of the limbs and metabolism*, it arrives in the domain of the will. It may be allowed to stimulate the *will* in the *limbs* in bound, controlled form, but must not enter directly into the metabolic processes. There it would be torn from its musical nature and would be effective directly in the metabolism and its chemical transformations, in other words it would unfold an *activity* withdrawn from human consciousness.

The threefold human being *in music* is portrayed by Steiner in a way that differs from the usual threefold depiction as regards the two extremes. Within music, the human being exists fully in the rhythmic system. Upwards one does not grasp the sphere of the senses (or only in a completely transformed inward form) though it is true one does grasp the nerve system of the head. Downwards one grasps the system of the limbs, but not the metabolic organism. Thus he remains more 'inward', he is not fully embodied within the physical body. It is the *ether body* in the human being, which shows this 'musical' configuration.

Similar to the human 'idol' mentioned earlier, there exist other such representations where the figure bears a head upon a long neck. The head, however, is hollow behind, and the countenance with a *nose*, very representative of all the senses, is turned upwards and so appears to be suspended from the heavens. The elongated trunk has rudimentary arms which are folded under the breast sharply emphasizing the middle realm. It continues below on extended, parallel legs whose feet are stretched downwards, consequently not walking but 'suspended'. This is a representation of the human etheric form, which corresponds to our 'music human being'.

What now are the three soul-members of the 'human being as music'? The middle member of the soul, *feeling*, is *harmony*. When harmony ascends to the head, which is otherwise the seat of concepts, it becomes *melody*. And only through melody is the head receptive to feeling. Melody consequently is the real *'bearer of meaning'* in music. When harmony descends into the limbs it becomes *rhythm*, which as 'will, taking its measured course in time' brings harmony, in other words the feeling which produces euphony, into human movement.

What does *harmony* do in its own realm? Here it reaches a faculty which otherwise is preserved only for thinking in the capacity of 'thinking about itself'. 'To feel feeling' is the soul-substance of music. This substance is at the same time active perception and perceptive doing. Like the most sensitive pair of balances, this feeling touches every fluctuation in the harmony of the psyche and changes it into sensitivity for sound. Every change of 'soul mood' is expressed in the change of mood of our inner instrument. We are 'tuned' happy or sad, 'in tune' or indeed 'out of tune' — our musical expression resounds correspondingly. And nothing is more dependent on the soul-body disposition, in other words our mood, than the singing voice, as every singer will confirm.

'Harmony' is not only the forming of chords. The task of this 'active feeling' is much more to bring the 'relationships', which are fundamental to everything musical, back into the right 'relationships' once again, and to reassert the ever-vacillating *balance* of these continually mobile 'members' of the being of music. Kepler called this sounding together the 'harmony of the universe', the concord of all relationships and motions of the heavenly spheres. 'Harmony' as chordal structure is only a few centuries old. It is in this sense 'congealed melody', the course of melodic movement squeezed into simultaneous sounding, in space, and hence into rhythms forced likewise into rigidity and one-offness. The chord is always something like a conclusion. It resembles a contention, a judgement.

In eurythmy, Steiner wished that the chord, this 'burial of melody', be released from its reciprocality into an arpeggio. On the coloured figures, which he gave for the major and the minor triad, on which are represented the key-note, third and fifth in their characteristic gestures, the designations are different from the descriptions in the lecture course. There the dress signifies *melos* instead of 'movement', the veil *rhythm* instead of 'feeling', and where the muscular tension calls up the character, stands *beat*. Here wonderful possibilities are given to practise the inner relationships and interpenetrations of musical forces. If harmony breaks forth, for example, into *melos*, then this becomes 'coloured', the minor lending it a different quality from the major. Gripped by the *minor* it glows crimson red, the burdening tendency of the minor renders it difficult to ascend, but glowing it plunges into the depths: 'like sparkling wine it flows through the veins'. [29] The major on the other hand lends *melos* the shining brightness of yellow-orange; it readily ascends; descent it does not like so much because it has to subdue its light, like the sun descending at sunset.

Rhythm inspired by the *minor* takes hold of all the short elements carried on the inbreathing stream of minor; it becomes rich, strong, almost gorgeous in intense orange. Longer notes which dissolve the rhythm are resisted by the insistence of the minor element. An inner struggle can be felt in the duration of the notes. But rhythm is breathed through by the *major*, it finds it easy to produce the long note, it feels it to be accepted in the cool, harmonious violet, and the fleeting of the short notes disappears before it.

Beat appears at last as the power of tension at those places on the figure where gestures commence, where they are supported. In the *major* it appears red, in other words effective outwardly, especially where it can make the figure appear large, stretched: where the shoulder is attached, at the shin and the dome of the head. When you follow this propulsion in movement, then movement striving outwards appears strong and radiant, the figure stands there like a spear-throwing warrior. Beat in the *minor* is green, calming, persistent. It is effective in the lower arms, in the thigh and in the lower jaw. It does not allow any extravagantly broad movement at all; if you wanted to give in to its retarding tendency you would have to sit down. The image of a splendid enthroned pharaoh appears, his arms resting on the supports of the throne, his heavy head with the Egyptian imperial beard solidly between his shoulders.

It is surely no coincidence that of all the musical elements, Steiner only indicated coloured images for the major and the minor triad. We have seen these form a sort of bridge to the realm of speech, which, making use of the colour, can 'appear on the human being'. It is strange that the harmonic sphere, which exists in the musical 'middle region', can also express its characteristic effect at the extreme 'periphery', where the domain of music borders on that of speech, and of colour. But 'harmony' is precisely the heart-force of music interpenetrating everything.

If we would follow up harmonic influences in the realm of the *intervals*, we experience how contemporary music elicits compromises from us. For *'actually'* every ascending interval is major, every descending one minor. So long as we remain in melody, this can be experienced. The increasing release of the ascending row of intervals does really have a 'major' character. A descending interval leads into inwardness, and consequently possesses a minor character. When, however, in our classical and romantic music the harmonic character of a specific key operates, it embraces everything in the cloak of *its* colour. Whether the melody rises or falls it remains dipped in the element of the respective key. [10]

In this world of keys, however, there is yet another effect of the power of 'harmony'. It can transform, it can create transitions, it can call forth modulations. It can convert major into minor and vice versa, it can carry us through the whole range of the circle of fifths or build daring bridges to new worlds. It is as though it were to lead us away from the earth and allow us to fly through the whole of space, always obeying laws and yet free to fashion as it will. What remains of the fundamental structure of tonic, subdominant and dominant? Yet harmony is ever and again the bridge to new doorways into new worlds, even when its form has been changed.

In this smelting furnace of harmony where everything is transmuted and renamed, the intervals likewise are caused to adopt ever new 'incarnations'. They serve as 'steps' in the literal sense, yet the steps themselves are recast, progressing from one function to another, till in this alchemical process they have become transmuted to gold, if the process has been spiritually genuine.

'To grasp the musical element, we have to enter into the spiritual realm.'

The primeval human being was created as an 'image of the gods' from the harmony of the cosmic spiritual forces, the 'cosmic Logos'. Here on earth an image of this cosmic human essence lives in the human etheric body. Descending into incarnation, the human being has gathered it together from all the spheres of the universe and brought it with him into his earthly body. He bears it within him as a 'being of time', as a complex of forces which makes possible the vital life-creating influence of time in his spatial corporeality. This being of time is not bound to an 'earlier' or 'later' time. In it the 'future in vital anticipation' (Goethe) exists and what came earlier is still thoroughly effective; past and future are both present in it to the same extent. This reciprocity, however, is not uniformity; on the contrary *everthing is possible* in infinite variety. [12]

This etheric body is the living *being* within us *that lives music*. Through its relationship with the cosmos, everything that the 'music of the spheres' has fashioned in it can resound in it, the laws of genesis as well as the prefiguring of the future.

We are able to 'experience' music when we submerge our ego into our *'starry body'*, into the astral body created from the cosmos according to musical laws. We ourselves are an instrument. The cosmos 'plays' our own being into existence. [30]

Musical laws are an expression of the genesis of the world and the coming into being of the human being: 'the developing drama of existence in sounds which are an external image for what the soul lives through consciously in the life of initiation'. [31]

To penetrate our ego into our astral body, which is equivalent to diving into the divine world, *is* the path through initiation. And music is a true image of this. Musical experience can become 'experiencing with the gods'.

Even that which is not yet here, what we shall experience only after death although we already carry it within us, we can fashion out of ourselves in musical creation, which is to create something that otherwise would not be here in the physical world. [32] In musical experience we step out of our everyday self, we dwell with the 'eternal' part of our being in that sphere of the universe where the creating of the gods, the life of the gods and the aims of the gods work in one stream.

The *archetype of the scale* resounds to us from *cosmic memory*. When we experience the descending evolution of Saturn, Sun and Moon in the first three notes: from above, from the zenith the gestures for the notes climb downwards (C,D,E) until they arrive on the earth in its first epoch, the Mars epoch (F). Now, however, the ascent ensues: the Mercury epoch, which is still an Earthly evolution (G), and then ascending further through the Jupiter, Venus, Vulcan evolutions (A,B,C). We have an inkling as to why it is necessary to present the gestures F and G in the form of a cross, for it is truly our Earthly epoch. We experience likewise how the power of will is appealed to in the feet (which indeed play a part with G,A,B), in order to turn round the direction of evolution, causing it to ascend. [33]

Our individual *human essence*, as it comes into being out of the cosmos every time our ego descends into incarnation, is depicted in the *scale:* the astral and etheric bodies accompany the *ego* as it takes hold of the *physical body*. Here the lowest notes of the scale resound. At the same time it is the limb pole of the human being. We live through the etheric body up to the middle of the scale, then through the upper notes of the scale into the region of the astral body and with the resounding of the octave arrive at the head, where the ego lights up in the waking experience of the senses. Our ego that we knew was working asleep in our physical body we have now refound in an awake state. And now we know: the head is octave of the feet. [34]

The archetype of our human essence, created by the stars, as it lives in our astral body, bears the inscription of the *sevenfold pattern* of our *essential human nature*. We rediscover it in the steps of the sevenfold *scale*.

In the *prime* the essence of our physical body resounds, as does that of the etheric body in the *second*, and the *third* expresses the double nature of our astral body: the *major* third the sentient body, the more inward *minor* third the sentient soul developing within it. In the *fourth*, which approaches the middle, the double countenance of the intellectual or mind soul is shown. In the *fifth* we grasp the consciousness soul, and in the three *higher degrees* we have an inkling of the influence of the future members of our being, the Spirit-self, the Life-spirit and Spirit-man. [35]

In this scale of the members of our being as it resounds in music, we witness the most wonderful differentiations. When we experience its harmony with the *kingdoms of nature* around us, we experience the ascent from solid to liquid, to aeriform to warmth, and here in the middle the transition from the kingdom of the elements or their aggregate (physical) condition to the world of the etheric forces, the warmth ether, the light ether, the sound or chemical ether, and to the life ether which penetrates everthing. [9]

Moreover, these qualitative experiences continue on in the field of the psyche. We can experience the scales as we live in two worlds, the inwardly physical and spiritual. [34] In the *fifth*, we experience a kind of midpoint, the ability to breathe in and out. In the *seventh* we experience a breathing out and are, in a way, out of ourselves. In the *third*, however, we breathe in, we go within ourselves. In the upper degrees of the scale we can come to conditions of soul which, subtly graded, correspond to the higher levels of knowledge, through which a 'leading out' of consciousness occurs. In the *fourth* we still experience the state of sense perception; the *fifth* shows us the state of Imagination, the sixth that of Inspiration; and in the seventh, where we break out of our own form, that of Intuition. (If we imagine what was said earlier about the interval returning to the fundamental, or key-note, then what has just been said might appear more immediately understandable.) [12]

Within the possibilities of our musical experience we also carry the echo of earlier human ways of experience, transformed to accord with the 'solidity' of our present state of incarnation and thus often having what could be called a different 'key signature'. Anthroposophy tells us about the level of consciousness of humanity in Atlantean times, indeed even in the *Lemurian* epoch. At that time when the 'inner being' still existed 'outside the human being', he could only live in tonal steps which were greater than our octave. The 'next' note was what we call a *ninth*, in other words the second over the octave. [36]

This, which for our present consciousness is hardly experienced as belonging together, was the smallest tonal step. In such cosmic dimensions the human being experienced the 'objective intervals'.

Then the human being stepped into earthly embodiment and experienced what we describe in the image of the fall of man. When a person of the following, *Atlantean* epoch experienced music, he felt carried away to the gods. Music was for him religious experience, the gods were revealed to him in sounds which we today would call *sevenths*. For the Altantean, the seventh was the smallest tonal step; his scale pulled him in giant steps out into an experience of the cosmos.

In the *first post-Altantean* epoch the human being experienced in the *fifth* an echo of the world of the gods. He felt himself already dwelling in his body in the fifth, however, the gods still lived around him. He felt himself carried up to them; he himself did not sing, 'the angel sang in him'.

Only in the fourth *post-Atlantean* epoch did the human being feel sufficiently connected with his physical configuration to be able to say 'I sing'. And now he enters into his soul in experiencing the *third*; no longer does he feel carried up to the gods in musical experience. He experiences his own essence, and how it can be expressed differently through the major and the minor third; his experience of destiny ran its course in the major and the minor.

We experience a contrast in these 'key signatures'. What was for the human being earlier an appropriate expression of his being, what appeared to him congenial is for us strange, unpleasant, irritating, for instance in the way the seventh affects us, or in the way the fifth feels empty to us. Our pathway leads ever more inwards, we try to achieve ever further differentiation. In our age (although the preference for thirds is still the rule) we are passing over more and more to the second, indeed even to the minor second. And are entering into a relationship with another interval which up to now has found no legitimate place in the scale, indeed in the Middle Ages it was 'forbidden' and was experienced as devilish, the *tritone*. This tonal step which divides the scale exactly into two halves, hence placing itself audibly where actually the gap should be, the free breathing space between the two tetrachords, is a typical expression of the intellectual age. It is a shrewd interval, an incision, and at the same time a materialization of what ought to remain immaterial, spiritual, free. This intermediate space which presents a caesura between the two worlds of experience in which the human being exists musically lies between the *fifth* and the *fourth*. And it is important to recognize the relationship between these two bases of the scale, namely that we stand with the fourth exactly on the boundary of our human configuration and look *inwards*. Whilst with the *fifth* we have 'human being becoming aware in the divine world-order', and in the third 'the human being becoming aware within himself', in the *fourth* we go about 'in the divine world as human beings beholding ourselves from outside.' [12]

Today, however, we do not yet experience the two 'corner pillars' of the scale, the key-note and the octave, as clearly differentiated as will be possible one day. Steiner frequently indicated that in the *single note* an experience of different nuances should be looked for; in the single note a kind of melody could be discovered, especially a trinity, the note that is, that was and that will be. Hence in the basic movement of the scale we should not remain with the *one* physically perceptible note, but learn to listen until we hear the etheric stream, the stream of time, with the present, past and future united in it. [20]

Then the future feeling for the octave will become possible as well, in which the human being grasps his ego outside himself once again, in that he discovers: 'I have now met my ego. 1 have been elevated in my humanity through the feeling for the octave.' It is a sublimated experience of metamorphosis, a transformation and at the same time a grasping in advance of the future which was there from the beginning – it corresponds precisely to the transformation of the fashioning forces of our body into the head forces of our next incarnation. Again we are able to perceive that the head is the octave of the feet. Therewith the musical experience has been transformed from an inner-outer experience to a time experience. This octave feeling could become for the human being in the future the proof for the existence of God, corresponding to the direct experience of the divine in music during primeval times.

From cosmic experience filled with the gods, as it still echoed on in the epoch of the fifth, the human being also gathered that wonderful image of the musical organism which we call the 'circle of fifths'. Through the range of the seven octaves which lie within human experience, the *fifth* presents itself *twelve times*. In the fifth the human being experienced his ego in movement still outside his physical system. Thus he could 'walk through' the seven octaves in twelve steps of fifths into the cosmos. From there he brought down with him the first seven fifths and united the five middle notes to a series: thus the pentatonic scale came into existence. Later he added the two corner pillars and our seven-note scale came into existence. [12]

The *key-note*, the *fourth* and the *fifth* as lower and upper dominants, have always had a special function in this musical cosmos: they were called 'the Mothers'. And they covernred music in the whole region of harmonic transformation. Between the sublime thrones of the 'Mothers', however, the other primal forces flow down bringing cosmic influences to humanity (*seventh* and *sixth*) and guiding it to our own organism (*third* and *second*). From these the wonderful tonal progression is composed which Steiner described as the TAO correspondence and which he fashioned into a meditation for eurythmists. [21]

With this exercise we stand again at a frontier of musical experience. We step on the bridge which leads us over into the realm of the word. As we described earlier in the 'inner space' of the harmonic world of major and minor experience, a possibility existed of giving expression to this experience with certain speech gestures. Similarly on the 'extreme frontier of the cosmos' we are able to produce a relationship to the realm of speech.

In the *concordance* of the scale with a certain sequence of vowels, correspondences and complements lie which can be made clearly visible in the gestures. When we change from the world of music to speech and back again, we create a continuous inversion of our consciousness for the reason that the sounds of speech appear *on* the human being but the musical sounds appear *through* the human being. [37] Thus through the gesture for the sounds of speech we are able to express the 'relationship of the human being to the world', and through the musical gesture his 'relationship as human being of soul and spirit to himself'. When we venture to push forward in the domain of speech via the vowel to the consonant corresponding to it and to arrive in the musical realm through the interval as far as the single note, then we really become, from practice producing this changing relationship, a traveller through different worlds. From the natural world of the consonants, through the feeling realm of the vowels the way leads over the frontier inwards into the soul realm of the intervals and further into the realm where the spiritually directed rays enter into the realm of the notes.

Here in active differentiation the dual being speech-music becomes one. The human being is 'completely contained in what he reveals in speech and music'. [38] He utters himself in this form of expression which is reserved for him alone. In his utterance through music and word the 'primal language' which actually was 'primal song' continues to resonate.

'Living with the gods'

In the ancient mystery tradition clairvoyant knowledge was called a 'musical knowledge'. [12] The genesis of the world, the development of humanity and the riddles of the human spirit are revealed through music.

'We are created by the gods out of the cosmos as astral beings. We ourselves are an instrument. The cosmos plays our own being.' We are able to 'lift up our astral being to such a sublime capacity of listening that we can hear the creative activity of the cosmic music'. [30]

'Experience of music lives in the inmost part of the human being, which does not belong at all to everyday consciousness, but has to do with what comes down from spiritual worlds, is incarnated and subsequently passes through death.' [12]

Our eternal entelechy originates in cosmic music. It knows that its homeland is in those spheres of the spiritual world to which it ascends every night in sleep and whence it brings ever again renewing forces into the day's awakening. In that world which it also reaches after death, every human spirit is a musical sound. Because of this the human being can become creatively active in the earthly world. [6]

'We already bear *within* us what our astral body only experiences after death. That is why it fashions in melody and harmony something out of itself which otherwise is not here in the physical world.' [32]

Musical experience is an experience of the whole human being, of how he lives in the earthly and in the heavenly world. He experiences himself linked to the universe, he feels himself as a microcosm in the macrocosm. [34]

'The musical element does not allow itself to be experienced as anything other than anthroposophical if you wish to experience it consciously.' [12]

But just as music is only really to be experienced through spiritual knowledge, it can also lead us on the way to initiation. It is with musical notes that the stars have created us. Through these notes we are able to seek our way to the stars.

With intensive practising we can penetrate into the experience of specific notes, specific intervals. They can become for us a window through which we are able to penetrate with our soul to a spiritual experience of what is behind the notes. [39] Music, with its dynamic, dramatic experiences of tension can be to us not merely an *image* of the pathway through initiation. We can experience its mighty power, like a catharsis, in the moral depths of our soul and it is even effective in the realm of health and illness, of chaos and harmony. [31]

The primal song of humanity was the speaking of the gods, musical experience was cosmic experience. Gods revealed themselves, and were present in tonal creations. Then for the human being the spiritual reality was lost and only the sound remained for him. [20, 12]

Here in the earthly realm air is the body of the sound. But sound itself is a spiritual entity. Only in the life after death can the human being live in the sound itself; he has the singing, the ensouled sounds of the universe *around* him. [38] He ascends through the starry universe until he penetrates so far 'that he beholds the stars from behind, and this beholding is at the same time a listening; resounding in the cosmic widths he hears the beings who have their dwelling in these cosmic bodies'.

What human beings experience *together with the gods*, when they find the way out of earthly experience, this they will relate in their musical creations'. [31]

And even the greatest and at the same time the most intimate spiritual event of earthly development, the descent of Christ into the earthly incarnation can be depicted through the deepened musical elements. 'Then the human being will be able to conjure up within the forming of sounds, in this formation of notes, something directly supersensible for musical feeling. The Christ-Impulse can be found in the sphere of music.' [40]

An immense future task for creators of music. How can music achieve this? It will be able to deliver the substances for it, for it is of a spiritual nature, its elements are in reality spiritual aspects of the being of music, essential aspects of the cosmic human archetype.

In the beginning was music. But it is always a force for the *future*. That is why it leads us into the stream of time, into the working of evolution. Movement and metamorphosis are its forms of expression. It is always in the process of becoming. Like the stream of life itself it is continuously active in creating and transforming. Even an (apparent) retreat is nevertheless a rushing forwards.

The past has led the visual arts to magnificent heights. The task for the future lies in the development of vital musical initiatives. If the visual arts are not to remain fixed or sink into degeneration, they have to be penetrated by the transforming powers of music. Architecture, sculpture and painting have to become flexible in their formations so that they can bring to expression the stream of time, the effect of the etheric. In experiencing architecture we shall develop musical moods. A reconciliation of the arts has to be striven for. 'The interpenetration of the visual arts and their formations with musical moods has to become absolutely the *artistic ideal of the future*. Music of the future will be more sculptural than music of the past. Architecture and sculpture of the future will become more musical than the architecture and sculpture of the past. That will be the essential thing. Music will not cease to be an autonomous art. It will only become richer because music will penetrate into the secrets of the notes and through this will create invisible forms out of the spiritual foundations of the cosmos.' [41]

In the First Goetheanum, Steiner realised artistically the principle of the future expressed by him in this way. In its architectural, sculptural forms, musical motivation was at work. The rigid material submitted itself to the flexible, forming stream of life. Space was interwoven and changed by time; it became an instrument. It resounded. It spoke.

'And the *Building becomes Man*.' [24] Our task as people of the Michael age is to bring again the temporal and what is supersensible everywhere into the realm of space'. In merely spatial images, in spatial conceptions the human being separates himself from the gods. When 'musical knowledge' carries the vital forces of anthroposophy into the rigid forms of our thinking and understanding, when not only the visual arts but also our whole culture is musically penetrated by spirit, when everything which has become spatially rigid has been brought again into movement by the vital stream of time, then human beings can be seized by the spiritual element, 'so that their life links directly with the divine life'. [42]

Everything frozen in form shall reappear in movement.

Everything hardened in material shall be penetrated again by the laws of life of the etheric realm.

Everything that has died in the intellect shall arise through the stream of life of spiritual wisdom in vital, mobile thoughts.

Thither we aspire through *art*.

Thither *music* and *eurythmy* are able to lead us.

> In art the human being redeems
> the spirit bound to the world;
> In the art of music,
> the spirit bound in himself.

> *In der Kunst erlöst der Mensch*
> *den in der Welt gebundenen Geist;*
> *In der musikalischen Kunst*
> *den in ihm selbst gebund'nen Geist.* [24]

Sources and Notes

In these annotations the sources are cited from which quotations are taken, or from which my own formulations are derived. Since I presume that most readers probably have access to the following two works, I give the reference to the respective lecture for everything quoted from there. These two works listed as GA 278 and GA 283 (see Bibliographic Survey, below) are *Eurythmy as Visible Music*, RSP London, 1977, o.p.; third edition, 'Eurythmy as Visible Singing', The Robinswood Press, Stourbridge (forthcoming) *(Ton-Eurythmie Kurs)*, henceforth referred to as GA 278, and the lectures *The Inner Nature of Music and the Experience of Tone*, AP New York, 1983 *(Das Tonerlebnis im Menschen)*, henceforth referred to as GA 283. References to other lectures are intended as stimulation and enrichment since they show supplementary aspects.

In this work we are dealing with the sources of experience of music, not with the intention of acquiring techniques of music eurythmy. Therefore I have not given descriptions of gestures, knowledge of which is presumed. Likewise I presume a knowledge of Steiner's spiritual-scientific expressions. Whoever is not familiar with these is referred to Steiner's fundamental works, *Theosophy* and *Occult Science – an Outline* (RSP London and AP New York).

(Translators' note: The following texts have been checked against the English versions where available but are all freshly worked. Two further quotations have been added for this edition under footnote 8.)

1. R. Steiner, Art as seen in the Light of Mystery Wisdom (lecture Dornach, 29.12.14) RSP London, 1984. GA 275:

'When we project the specific laws of the human body into space outside it, then we have architecture... If we seek the laws of sculpture we must realise that they are in fact the laws of our etheric body... If we push what is in us of an astral nature a step lower down into the etheric body... Painting is born... If...we descend with the ego into the astral body: then music is born.'

2. R. Steiner, Eurythmy as Visible Music (lecture Dornach, 23.2.24) RSP London, 1977:

'The Goetheanum was musical, and the Goetheanum was eurythmical'.

R. Steiner, Ways to a New Style in Architecture (lecture Dornach, 23.2.24) Anthroposophical Publishing Co., London 1927. GA 286:

'You will understand what we intended by this building when you start wanting to understand the spirit which has the power to impress itself with what surrounds as the outer shell of the building. You will then see in the artistically impressed forms around you the impress of what has to be accomplished and proclaimed in living words in our building. It is a living Word this building of ours!'

> R. Steiner, Art as seen in the Light of Mystery Wisdom (lecture Dornach, 2.1.15) RSP London, 1984. GA 275:

'We become aware, too, that whereas outside, the architectural element is supporting, weighing down and creating a balance, we ourselves in this encounter with the architectural element develop a musical mood. Our inner being attunes itself musically in accordance with this architecture, and we notice that even though the elements of architecture and music appear to be so alien to one another in the outer world, through this musical mood engendered in us, our experience of architecture brings about a reconciliation, a balance between these two elements.

This is where, from our epoch onwards, living progress in the arts will lie, through learning to experience the reconciliation of the arts... Reconciling the arts: that is what we attempted to do (for the first time, and in a small, elementary way) in our Goetheanum building. We did not want only to talk in a cold, prosaic way about it, but to show in the architecture of the building itself an impression, a copy of this reconciling of a musical mood with architectural form... We attempted to bring architectural forms into musical flux, and the feeling you can have from seeing the interplay between the pillars and all that is connected with them, can of itself arouse a musical mood in the soul. It is possible to feel invisible music as the soul of the columns and the architectural and sculptural forms that belong to them. The soul element is in them, so to speak.'

> R. Steiner, *Das Goetheanum in seinen zehn Jahren. Goethe und Goetheanum* [The Goetheanum in the ten years of its life], Dornach 1961, GA 36:

'When the art of eurythmy appeared on the stage of the Goetheanum, people were to have the feeling that the resting forms of the interior architecture and the sculpture were related in quite a natural way to the human beings as they moved... The building and the movements of eurythmy were intended to grow together to a whole... And when the architectural forms of the stage received the fashioning of eurythmy, as it were, as something belonging to them, so did those forms in the auditorium receive the recitation or declamation appearing parallel with the eurythmy... Such a unity of building-form and word or music was *striven for*... The attempt was made to fashion in such a way that you could feel how the movement of the word naturally ran along the forms of the capitals and architraves. I wish only to indicate with this what can be attempted with such a building, that its forms do not merely externally enclose the things presented therein, but give an immediate impression of *containing* them in a living whole.'

3. See lectures 3-6 in GA 278.

R. Steiner, *The Renewal of Education* (lecture Dornach, 16.5.20), Steiner Schools Fellowship, 1981. GA 301:

'In the true musical element we have an expression of the human soul only. All that ultimately manifests in the musical element has really only in the most rudimentary way an analogy in outer nature such as we have in modelling, painting and drawing. With the musical element it would not even be possible in the same way to wish merely to imitate the external world naturalistically, as is possible in a time when artistic feeling for drawing or modelling is weak, merely imitating the external world. Yet is music devoid of content? It certainly has content! The essential content of music is the melodic element. Melodies have to come as inspiration. If nowadays in many quarters the melodic element is not valued so highly, it is just another sign of our materialistic age. People are just not imaginative enough. It is the melodic element that is the genuine content of music. Where does the melodic element originate? The melodic element can well be compared with the sculptural element. The sculptural element is related, is it not, to space as is the melodic element to time. Anyone who has a keen sense for this temporal orientation will recognize that a kind of 'temporal sculpture' is contained in the melodic element...

What lies at the root of dreams, this increasing and fading away of feelings, these tensions and, perhaps, resolutions, or the inclination to some kind of feeling which leads to a calamity...compare this in all earnestness with what lies at the root of the musical element. Then you have in the dream-pictures only something irregular; in the musical element you have something that presents itself in exactly the same way in increasing and fading-away and so on... Melodies enter as reminiscences into our daily life. People recognize so little the real origin of musical themes because what is expressed in the musical themes they experience in the time between falling asleep and awakening. For the human being today this is present as a still unconscious element revealing itself only when in dreams it forms pictures. This unconscious element, however, which operates in the dream and which works precisely in the melodic element, this unconscious element we have to get hold of in the art of teaching, in order that we can get beyond materialism through the art of education...

And melodies are there, whence we know not. In reality they emanate from the realm of sleep. In reality we experience temporal sculpture between falling asleep and waking up... Few people recognize that a sentence consisting of a subject, verb and object is really a melody in the unconscious. Just as we can call to mind that what we experience in sleep as an increasing and fading-away of feelings, like a graph depicting feelings, rises up into consciousness clothed in images, so we experience the sentence musically in the depths of our being. And since we adapt ourselves to the world, we clothe the musically felt experience with the sculptural image. "The child writes his essay" – subject – verb – object. A triad, a common chord, is experienced in our innermost depths.'

4. Goethe, 'On Art'. in Spruche in Prosa [Prose aphorisms].

5. R. Steiner 'Uber die Gruppen – Iche von Tieren, Pflanzen und Minerallen' [On the group-egos of animals, plants and minerals] (Lecture, Frankfurt 2.2.08, answers to questions). In the supplement to Das Goetheanum 1945, 22nd year, no 22.

'Question: What are the Logoi? Answer: A most comprehensive understanding is necessary in order to appreciate the Logoi... When we read in the beginning of John's Gospel: In the beginning was the Word (the Logos), then we gradually acquire an inkling about it... The earth, so far as we are able to look back, has passed through three embodiments: Saturn, Sun, and Moon. The Sun at that time was a planet. Today's sun has evolved to a ... fixed star out of the earlier planet 'Sun'. When our Earth comes to be embodied as 'Venus', then by that time it will be approaching a Sun existence. *The Earth will become a Sun. And what will ultimately result from a Sun? Out of a sun a Zodiac will ultimately come into existence*... When our Earth was 'Saturn', Words of highly developed beings resounded from the Zodiac down to the earth. And the Words were creative. Development proceeds ever higher until man himself will become a being who creates through the Word. Thus we gain a feeling for how the human being will become a creative Logos and how he proceeded from the creating Logos. When we imagine this, then we have raised ourselves to what is called the third Logos. It is cosmic sound, which resounds through the universe from the Beings who through the Word have become creative.'

6. R. Steiner, lecture Cologne 3.12.06 in GA 283:

'For those who care to reflect on it, music has always been something of an enigma from the aesthetic point of view. On the one hand, music is most readily comprehensible to the soul, to the immediately sensitive realm of human feeling; on the other hand, it also presents difficulties for those wishing to grasp its effects. If we wish to compare music with the other arts, we have to say that all the other arts actually have models in the physical world... Someone who wishes to apply this approach to music, however, is hardly likely to come to any results as all... Whence actually do artistically fashioned notes come and upon what are they related to in the world?... The reason why the musical element can speak to everyone, why it affects the human being from earliest childhood, becomes comprehensible to us from the realm of existence where the true models of music live. When the musician composes he cannot imitate anything. He has to draw the motifs of his music from his soul. To discover whence he draws them we have to refer to worlds that are imperceptible to the senses. We have to consider how these higher worlds are actually constituted. The human being is capable of opening up higher faculties in the soul which otherwise slumber.'

There follows a description of the stages of development: experience of the ocean of colours of the astral world, then of Devachan (Spirit-land).

'In this state of consciousness the human being achieves the faculty to hear spiritually, to perceive tonal combinations, manifold tonal structures, which are inaudible to the physical ear. This world is called Devachan. Now, you should not imagine that when the human being hears the spiritual world of musical sound welling up that he does not retain the world of light and colours too. The world of sound is also permeated by light and colours belonging to the astral world. The most characteristic element of the Devachanic world, however, is this flowing ocean of musical sounds. Out of this world of the continuity of consciousness the human being can fetch the resounding element and thus hear it in the physical world. A musical sound lies at the foundation of everything in the physical world. All objects possess a spiritual sound at the foundation of their being, and the human being himself in his deepest essence is such a spiritual sound... Each time the human being falls asleep and loses consciousness, his astral body departs from his physical body. Then the human being is unconscious, it is true, though living in the spiritual world. The spiritual sounds make an impression on his soul. Every morning the human being awakens from the world of the music of the spheres, and out of this realm of beautiful harmony he re-enters the physical world. If it is true that man's soul experiences Devachan between two embodiments, then we may also say that the soul during the night feasts on and lives in flooding sound as the element out of which it is actually woven, which is actually the soul's homeland.

The creative musician transposes the rhythm, the harmonies and melodies that are impressed in his etheric body during the night into physical notes. Unconsciously the musician has received the prototype of the spiritual world which he transposes into physical sounds. This is the mysterious relationship between music that resounds here in the physical world, and hearing spiritual music in the night. A person illuminated by light casts a shadow on the wall. The shadow is not the real person. Likewise music produced in the physical world is a shadow, a real shadow of a much loftier music of Devachan. The archetype, the pattern of music is in Devachan, physical music is but a reflection of the spiritual reality... When the human being lives within the musical element, he lives in a reflection of his spiritual home. In this shadow image of something spiritual, the human soul finds its highest exaltation, the most intimate relationship to the primal human element. That is why even the simplest soul is so deeply affected by music. Even the simplest soul feels in music an echo of what it has experienced in Devachan. The soul feels at home there... From this intuitive recognition Schopenhauer assigned the central position among the arts of music and said that in music the human being perceives the heartbeat of the will of the world.'

R. Steiner, (lecture Berlin, 12.11.06), ibid.:

'The special characteristic of Devachan, is that it is a sounding world at least its essence... Of course, this world is shone through by the astral world from which it is not separated. The astral world permeates the Devachanic world... Essentially, however, the Devachanic realm is tonal... On a still higher plane of Devachan the musical sound becomes something akin to words... Now we have to bear in mind that not only the initiate lives in these worlds. The only difference is that the initiate undergoes these various altered conditions consciously. The states the ordinary person repeatedly undergoes unconsciously, are changed into conscious ones for him. For in actual fact the ordinary person passes through these three worlds time and again, only he knows nothing about it because he is not conscious of himself or of his experiences there. Nevertheless, he returns with some of the effects that these experiences called forth in him. When he awakens in the morning not only is he physically rejuvenated by sleep but he brings art from these worlds as well... We see in painting the shadow, the precipitation, of the astral world in our physical world. The musician, on the other hand, conjures up a still higher world; he conjures the Devachanic world right into the physical world. In actual fact melodies and harmonies which speak to us from the works of the great masters are faithful copies of the Devachanic world.'

R. Steiner, *The Influence of Spiritual Beings Upon Man* (lecture Berlin 11.06.08) AP New York, 1961, GA 102:

Forces which the soul brings over from the world of sleep: 'All these forces proceeding here and there in space, which a person feels so easily in space, are realities, actualities, and from this feeling for space all architecture proceeds... These are the forces becoming effective in us and which are perceived in the physical body as a feeling-of-ourselves in space. The true artist experiences space in this way and fashions it architecturally.

Turning now to the etheric body, we have once again what the inwardness of the soul assimilates nocturnally in the spiritual world and brings with it when it slips back into the etheric body. What is expressed thus in the etheric body is perceived by the true sculptor... When the inwardness of soul meets with the soul-body there arises in the same way the feeling for the line, for the first elements of painting. And through the fact that in the morning the sentient-soul is united with the soul-body, permeating it, harmony of colour arises... Now since the intellectual or mind-soul takes flight every night in the astral world, something else again comes about...'intellect', as understood by spiritual science, is the sense for harmony which cannot be embodied in external matter, the sense for inwardly experienced harmony...Now when the intellectual or mind-soul dips into the harmonies of the astral world every night and in the morning becomes conscious of it in the astral body then the following occurs: In the night the intellectual or mind-soul lives in what has always been called the harmony of the spheres... The soul exists in these resounding spheres during the night... All these things that humanity knows as the art of music are the expressions, impressions of what is experienced in the harmony of the spheres, and to be musically gifted means nothing other than to possess an astral body which during the day is receptive for what hums through it all night long... What the human being experiences in the art of music is the sounding in of a spiritual world.'

> R. Steiner, *Meditatively acquired Knowledge of Man* (lecture Stuttgart 10.9.20) Steiner Schools Fellowship 1982. GA 302a:

Music is physical by being a reflection in the air of the music of the spheres. Air serves as the medium through which the sounds become physical...; whereas what is not physical in the music-air is what unfolds its true effect only after death... with this we work into the future.

7. R. Steiner, *The Influence of Spiritual Beings upon Man* (lecture Berlin 16.03.08). GA 102:

'Sound arose, came into being (sound as such) side by side with the formation of water. And just as the air was filled with streams of light, so then the whole of the water to which the air had condensed...had waves of sound vibrating through it. On earth then precisely those parts where it was most watery were penetrated by harmonies of the spheres... You have to imagine here, of course, that in this primeval water...all the substances were contained which today are separated out as metals, minerals, and so on. It is especially interesting...to see how the most differing forms are formed from the water, because the sound creates forms in water... And the most important formation created by the dance of substances to the music of the cosmos is protein, protoplasm...primeval protoplasm, protein, was created from the cosmic substance, which was created out of the harmonies of cosmic music.'

R Steiner, *Meditatively acquired Knowledge of Man* (lecture Stuttgart 16.9.20). GA 302a:

'A mysterious music pours through everything that takes place in nature: the earthly projection of the music of the spheres. A sound of the music of the spheres is indeed incorporated in every plant, in every animal. This is even the case with regard to the human body, but not as far as human speech is concerned, not in the expressions of the soul, that is, but certainly with regard to the body and its forms, and so on...'

'A person who views a human skeleton with truly psycho-somatic vision...will see incorporated in the skeleton a musical achievement, which runs its course in the interaction between the human organism and the outer world. The human skeleton can be understood figuratively as if someone were playing a sonata and preserving it through some sort of spiritual process of crystalization; if we were to do this we come upon the principle forms, the arrangement of forms of the human skeleton!'

R. Steiner, *'Die Apokalypse'*, (lecture Munich, 8.5.07) in the supplement to *Das Goetheanum* 1945, 22nd year, no 19:

'What proceeds from the *seven planets* sounds right into our etheric body. A sevenfold influence on the etheric body is present, like the seven notes: prime, second, third, fourth, fifth, sixth, seventh. Saturn, Sun, Moon, Mars, Mercury, Jupiter, Venus. These seven planets resound into our etheric bodies. Twelve influences resound into the physical body, proceeding from the Zodiac. The seer discovers twelve fundamental notes on the Devachanic plane. These influence our physical body. Everything that exists in the ego, in the astral body, in the etheric body, and in the physical body resounds in notes.

        1 note sounds into the ego
        3 notes sound into the astral body
        7 notes sound into the etheric body
        12 notes sound into the physical body.

Together this yields a harmony, or else a disharmony. According to an occult expression: the 12 goes over into the 7, which means: the physical body becomes ever more similar to the etheric body. If the physical body is resounding properly, we hear through the 12 notes, the 7 notes of the stars.'

See also in R. Steiner, *Background to the Gospel of St Mark* (lecture Berlin, 7.3.11) RSP London, 1968. GA 124:

'What sets the muscle into motion, what calls up some movement or other in the muscle, concerns the astral body, and in fact in the astral body itself a kind of note production, a kind of sound production occurs to the movement of the muscle. Something akin to music pervades our astral body and the expression of this note production is the movement of the muscle. It really resembles what we know as the Chladni sound patterns when light, mobile powder or sand is scattered on a metal plate: when we draw a violin bow across the edge we get a pattern. Our astral body, too, is permeated with a number of such patterns (which are, however, patterns of notes) which work together so that our astral body assumes a specific condition. It is impressed into the astral body... Thus we are filled with music and bring it to life in the movements of our muscles. And we have the motor nerves, wrongly so-called, in order to have some awareness of the motions of our muscles.'

See Ernst Florens Chladni (1756-1827), *Die Akustik*, Leipzig, 1802 [and Mary Desiree Walker *Chladni Figures, A Study in Symmetry* (London, Bell, 1961) (Translators' note)].

8. R. Steiner, (lecture Stuttgart 7.3.23) in GA 283:

'It is hardly possible to discuss the musical element in the concepts to which we are accustomed in ordinary life. The reason is simply that the musical element really does not exist in the physical world given to us... Musical experience involves the whole human being, and the function of the ear in musical experience is completely different from what is normally assumed. Nothing is more incorrect than the simple statement: 'I hear a note, or I hear a melody with my ear'. That is completely wrong. A note or a melody or some harmony or other is actually experienced by the whole human being. And this experience reaches our consciousness through the ear in quite a particular way. Notes which we normally deal with have the air as their medium, as you know. Even if we use an instrument other than a wind instrument, the element in which the note exists is still the air. But what we really experience in the note has actually nothing more to do with the air. In fact the ear is that organ which before we hear the note, first separates the air element from the note, so that we receive the note, in that we experience it as such, as a resonance, or a reflection.

The ear is actually that organ which throws the airborne note back into the inner being of man in such a way that it separates out the air element; then, in that we hear it, the note lives in the etheric element. In other words, the ear is actually there (if I may put it like this) to overcome the resounding of the note in the air and to throw the pure etheric experience of the note back into our inner being.'

R. Steiner, *The Renewal of Education* (lecture Basel 21.4.20) Steiner Schools Fellowship, 1981. GA 301:

'The cerebro-spinal fluid moves from the brain rhythmically up and down the spinal chord, spreading then into the abdominal region, becoming pushed back into the cerebral ventricles with inhalation, and then forced out and with the exhalation flows downwards once again. This cerebro-spinal fluid, or rather its continuation into the rest of the organism, is in continuous movement up and down, so that an ever vibrating movement occurs, which... fills the entire human being and is connected with breathing. Now, when we are listening to a progression of notes, we are breathing... and when we hear, the rhythm of the rising and falling fluid strikes against what is formed there in us in the organ of hearing as sense perception through the notes, and a continuous striking together of the inward vibration-music of our breathing takes place with what the process of perception strikes on our ears. The actual musical experience consists in this balancing between the aural perception and the rhythmical breathing process.

R. Steiner, *Kunst und Kunst erkenntnis*, 'Art and its appreciation', (lecture Vienna 1.6.18). GA 271:

'We think that when we enjoy music our ears are involved and perhaps the nervous system of our brain, but that is only a superficial way of viewing the process...Something quite different from the merely aural process or what happens in our brain forms the basis here. What is at the root of musical feeling can be presented thus: each time we breathe out, the brain, the inner region of the head, allows its cerebro-spinal fluid to descend through the spinal chord down to the diaphragm. The opposite occurs when breathing in: the cerebro-spinal fluid is pushed against the brain. A continuous rhythm, a rising and falling fluctuation of the cerebro-spinal fluid takes place... This cerebro-spinal fluid fluctuates up and down in the arachnoid space [cerebral ventricles – Translators' note] in expansions which are more or less elastic so that the rising and falling of the cerebro-spinal fluid flows into the elastic and less elastic parts. This gives a quite wondrous kind of effect within a rhythm. The whole human organism apart from the head and limbs is expressed in this inner rhythm. What streams in through the ear as sound, what lives in us as tonal representation, becomes music by meeting the inner music which is produced because the whole organism is a remarkable musical instrument...

If I were to describe everything I would have to tell you of a wonderful inner human music, which actually is not heard but is inwardly experienced. What is experienced is basically nothing but a meeting with an inner singing of the human organism. This human organism, precisely in regard to what I have now described, is the image of the macrocosm. In the most definite laws, more strict than natural laws, we carry this Apollo's lyre within us, upon which the cosmos plays in us... Our organism...is the most wonderful musical instrument.'

> R. Steiner, *The Arts and Their Mission* (lecture Dornach 2.6.23) AP New York. GA 276:

'With music... we enter directly into that which the soul experiences as the spiritual or pyscho-spiritual: we leave space entirely. Music is linear, one-dimensional; it is experienced one-dimensionally in the thread of time. In music the human being experiences the world as his own. The soul does not assert something it needs upon descending into or leaving the physical world; rather it experiences something which lives and vibrates here and now, on earth, in its own soul-spirit nature. By studying the secrets of music, we can discover what the Greeks, who knew a great deal about these matters, meant by the lyre of Apollo. What is experienced musically is really the human being's hidden adaptation to the inner harmonic-melodic relationships of cosmic existence out of which he was fashioned. His nerve fibres, ramifications of the spinal cord, are marvellous musical strings with a metamorphosed activity. The spinal cord culminating in the brain, and distributing its nerve fibres throughout the body, is the lyre of Apollo. Upon these nerve fibres the soul-spirt man is "played" within the earthly world. In this world the human being himself is the most perfect instrument, and the notes of an external musical instrument are conjured up artistically to the degree that he feels this connection between the sounding of strings of a new instrument, which has to do with his own coursing blood and nerve fibres. The human being, as nerve-man, is inwardly built up of music, and he feels music artistically to the degree that he feels its harmonization with the mystery of his own musical structure.

Thus, in devoting himself to the musical element, the human being appeals to his earth-dwelling soul-spirit nature. The discovery by anthroposophical vision of the mysteries of this nature will have a fructifying effect not just on theory, but upon actual musical creation.'

> R. Steiner, ibid. (lecture Oslo 18.5.23)

'Now if we enter man's inner nature, we find something set against the external world-configuration: a marvellous harmony between the breath rhythm and blood rhythm. The rhythm of breathing (a human being normally breathes eighteen times per minute) is transferred to man's nerves, becomes motion. Physiology knows very little about this process. The rhythm of breathing is contained in the nerve system in a delicate pyscho-spiritual manner.

As for the blood rhythm, it originates in the metabolic system. In an adult four pulse beats normally correspond to one breath rhythm; seventy-two pulse beats per minute. What lives in the blood, that is, the ego, the sunlike nature in the human being, plays upon the breathing system and, through it, upon the nervous system... Now look at the spinal chord, its nerves extending in all directions, observe the blood vessels, and become aware of an inward playing of the whole sun-implanted blood system upon the earth-given nervous system. The Greeks with their artistic natures were aware of this interrelation. They saw the sun-like nature in man, the playing of the blood system upon the nervous system, as the god Apollo; the spinal cord with its wonderful ramification of strings, upon which the sun principle plays, as Apollo's lyre. Just as we meet architecture, sculpture, the art of costuming and painting when we approach the human being from the external world, so we meet music, rhythm, beat, when we approach the inner human being and trace the marvellous artistic forming and stirring which take place between blood and nerve system. Compared to external music, that performed between blood and nerve system in the human organism is of far greater sublimity...'

> R. Steiner, *First Scientific Lecture Course* (lectures Stuttgart, 30 and 31.12.19) Goethean Science Foundation, 1949. GA 320:

'We have to partake, too, in the element of air, we ourselves have to have something airy differentiated within us, so that we can perceive a resounding instrument, the external, differentiated airy element. [You] perceive the note or sound in question through the interaction of your inner, wonderfully constructed musical instrument with what is manifested externally in the air as notes, as sound. The ear is to a certain extent merely the bridge through which your inner Apollo's lyre interchanges... with what approaches you from without as differentiated movement of the air.'

> R. Steiner, ibid. lecture 31.12.19:

'So as far as listening is concerned, the ear has no reality at all... What is transmitted through the ear to the inwardness of soul must first... enter into a reciprocal relationship with the inner rhythm as it runs its course and becomes apparent in the rise and fall of the cerebro-spinal fluid... In their inner reality vibrations of the air have nothing to do with notes, except that where these vibrations of the air take place, a suction process arises in order to draw the notes in.'

R. Steiner, *The Wisdom of Man* (lectures Berlin, 23, 25 and 26.10.09) AP New York 1971. GA 115:

23.10.09:

'The note causes the inner nature of objects to vibrate... Through the intimate sense of hearing... you perceive the way in which the object is inwardly mobile. We distinguish among objects according to their inner nature, how they are able inwardly to quiver and vibrate, when we cause them to resound. In a way the soul of objects speaks to us here.'

25.10.09:

'Now we return to the domain which we call the sense of hearing. Here the etheric body is involved... The human being has to be permeated by beings who place at his disposal their own substance... The beings we call Angeloi... send their astral substance into us human beings... It streams through our ears to meet what is carried to us by the note. As it were, on the wings of these beings we enter into that inwardness which we learn to recognize as the soul of the objects.'

For the sense of sound *Lautsinn*, and the sense of thought/concept *Vorstellungssinn* – melody, harmony, overtones – see lecture of 26.10.09.

R. Steiner, 'The Ear' (lecture Stuttgart, 9.12.22) *Golden Blade*, London 1970. GA 218:

'The inner form of an eye, the inner form of an ear, are produced from the work which the human being accomplishes between death and a new birth in co-operation with supersensible spiritual beings. For this reason we can say: When we observe a human eye we should not assert that this human eye is comprehensible, like a crystal of salt, from what can be perceived around us, or that the ear is to be understood from what can be perceived around us. Rather we have to say: If we want to understand a human eye, or a human ear, then we must have recourse to those secrets which we can ascertain in the supersensible world. We have to be clear that a human ear (to remain with this example) is fashioned from the supersensible world and that only after it is fashioned does its task as a sense organ within the sphere of the air commence, or indeed within the sphere of the earth in general, namely, to hear notes or sounds in a physical way...

When you consider the human ear in its inner formation, then initially when you look down the external ear canal, you meet what we term the ear-drum. Behind this ear-drum sit small, tiny little bones; ordinary physiology speaks of hammer, anvil, stirrup-bone (*malleus, cacus, stapes*)... I will now observe the ear from within outwards and then you can see that what rests on the inner part of the inner ear, called in biology the stirrup-bone, looks like a transformed or metamorphosed human thigh-bone with its attachment at the hip. And what physiology calls the anvil, this tiny little bone, looks like a transformed knee-cap, and what reaches then from this anvil to the ear-drum looks like a transformed shin-bone with the foot attached. And the foot stands in this case not on the ground, but on the ear-drum. You have in actual fact a human limb in the interior of the ear, it is a transformed limb... And just as you feel the ground with your two legs, so do you touch the ear-drum with the foot of this tiny bone of the ear...

Even further within you find the cochlea, or 'snail-shell'. This is filled with a fluid. All this is necessary for hearing. What the 'foot' investigates on the ear-drum has to be transmitted inwards towards this scroll lying inside the ear cavity. The intestines are situated above the thigh. The scroll in the ear is a very finely formed intestine, a transformed intestine. Thus actually you could really imagine a human being in the ear. Its head is immersed in our own brain. Indeed we bear a whole number of more or less metamorphosed human beings within us... The human being could even develop in such a way that he not only possesses an ear here and another here, but might perhaps have one down below. This would be a paradox, certainly, however this paradox is completely true. The human being could become an ear down below too. Why, then, does he not become an ear down below? He does not become an ear because at a specific stage of his embryonic development he arrives in the region of earthly gravity... The ear that wants to grow downwards becomes, under the influence of earthly gravity, the lower part of the body...

The music of the spheres is a reality, and as soon as we arrive in the spiritual world which lies behind the soul world, we find ourselves in a world which lives altogether in speech sounds and notes in melody and harmony and concords of sounds. And out of these connections of speech sounds and harmonies the human ear is formed. For this reason we can say that in our ear we have a memory of our spiritual, pre-earthly existence; in the lower human system we have forgotten our pre-earthly existence, and the organism is adapted to earthly gravity, to all that results from weight... But just as the lower human being, as he stands on the earth with his legs, is transformed from an incipient ear so is everything moral which has come about through walking, whether you have proceeded to good or bad deeds, transformed, after the human being has passed through the gate of death (not straightaway but after a while) into notes and sounds... Your moral deeds become beautiful music, your immoral deeds become ugly music. And out of the concordant and discordant notes the Words, spoken by the higher hierarchies as judges over your deeds, will be heard by you...

That we see, hear, smell, taste and so on, is sense perception, and the organs of this sense perception, which lie on the outer periphery of our organism, are fashioned out of the highest spiritual regions. The ear is fashioned out of the music of the spheres. The ear is so strongly formed from the music of the spheres that it remains protected from gravity. The ear is also so disposed in the fluid that gravity cannot reach it; this ear is really not a citizen of the earth, in its whole organization it is a citizen of the highest spiritual worlds.'

9. R. Steiner, *Okkulte Zeichen und Symbole* (Occult signs and symbols), lectures Cologne, 28 and 29.12.07. In the supplement to *Das Goetheanum*, 1948, 25th year, nos. 33, 38, 39.

28.12.07:

'Images (symbols) lead the human being to participate in the world immediately bordering his. If we would enter into a still higher world we would be dealing no longer with mere images but with the inner relationship of images which is called the harmony of the spheres, music of the spheres... It is not with your ears that you hear the world of Devachan... We cannot compare the nature of the real world of sounding... with our physical notes... Spiritual notes are the substances of the spiritual world. The world of images leads over to the world of sounds; you see these worlds really do play into each other. Here, all around the physical world, the astral and Devachanic worlds exist at the same time; one interpenetrates the other... And you perceive everything present in the one world in the other too. What is spiritual music in the world of Devachan is shadowed in the astral world and is expressed there through numbers and figures... What we normally call Pythagorean music of the spheres... is a true reality... In the interplay between the planets of our solar system... we have given an expression of the spiritual world, that which perceives hears the reciprocal relations of the movements of our planets. For spiritual observation Saturn, for example, moves $2\frac{1}{2}$ times faster than Jupiter – the measurements are specified from the point of view of the higher world. This movement of Saturn... is perceived in the spiritual world as a correspondingly higher note... Now let us... imagine for ourselves the relationships of the movements in our solar system... For those who observe from a spiritual viewpoint, the whole movement of our accessible, visible stars in relationship to what we consider as their background... the whole starry heavens shifts forwards just one degree every century:

Saturn : Jupiter	=	$2\frac{1}{2}$	: 1
Jupiter : Mars	=	5	: 1
Sun, Mercury, Venus : Mars	=	2	: 1
Sun, Mercury, Venus : Moon	=	12	: 1
Saturn : fixed stars	=	1200	: 1

These ratios are expressed for spiritual perception by the sounds which are perceived in the spiritual world by the spiritual ear. This is what is really meant by the term 'music of the spheres' and these numbers in actual fact specify for you the harmonies really present in the spiritual world — brought about by what underlies our planetary system as the spiritual element...

Just as the clairvoyant sees images and colours in the astral world, so the clairaudient person hears in the spiritual world, or world of Devachan, the spiritual backgrounds of the objects... Everything which is revealed here in the physical world produces notes when you relate it to its spiritual background... The result... of the tonal vibrations of earth, water, air, fire is portrayed in the original form of a musical instrument, in the lyre. In the lyre the ratios of the vibrations of its strings are copied from the notes which the initiates knew for the four elements; thus

> bass string (E) corresponds to earth,
> G string   fire,
> A string   air,
> D string   water,

... Everything which occurs in the human being (in the microcosmos) should be imitated in concord with everything which occurs spiritually in the macrocosmos... then universe and man harmonize.'

29.12.07:

'The human being has to learn to feel the inner ratios of the numbers like a spiritual music... Imagine a note which makes three vibrations to a certain period of time, another note which makes seven vibrations and another which in the same period makes twelve vibrations. In these tonal vibrations you have an expression of the ratio which in spiritual music shows the relationship of ego = 1, astral = 3, ether body = 7, physical body = 12. There is good reason for this in universal existence... In its first embodiment, that of Saturn, the earth was surrounded by the twelve signs of the Zodiac. In their influence upon Saturn these gave the first germinal stage of the physical body. The seven planets influenced the etheric body. When the earth was Sun, the other planets were situated around the earth and thus they worked in a sevenfold way. When the earth was Old Moon... when the sun and the moon were removed from the earth, three bodies arose out of one. Thus the number 3 had influence on the formation of the astral body. When the ego descended from higher worlds, this was expressed in the number 1. The ratios 1:3:7:12 give you what you have to feel inwardly as the relationship between the four members of the human being.'

R. Steiner, *Okkulte Sinnbilder und Zeichen* (Occult symbols and signs) lecture Stuttgart, 13.9.07. In the supplement to *Das Goetheanum*, 1948, 25th year, no 18:

'We know that the earth revolves around the sun, that Mercury and Venus, as siblings of the earth do likewise; we know that the sun itself also moves. Occult astronomy has engaged in very exact research into this. It has investigated not only the movement of the earth and the other planets but also the movement of the sun itself, and here we arrive at a definite point in space, a kind of spiritual midpoint around which the sun, and with it our earth and all the planets, turns. The different bodies do not move at the same velocity; occult astronomy has established the relationship between these velocities of their movements to each other. It proceeded from the fact that all these heavenly bodies move with a certain velocity, while the whole world of fixed stars is apparently still, without motion... In reality the fixed stars move in 100 years by a certain amount, and this amount by which they move is taken as the cardinal number. If you assume this movement and compare the motions of the planets with it, then the following results: the movement of Saturn is 2½ times as quick as that of Jupiter, that of Jupiter 5 times as quick as that of Mars, that of Mars 2 times as quick as that of the Moon. The movement of Saturn, however, is 1200 times as quick as the whole background of the fixed stars.

When a physical musical harmony arises, this touches on the fact that... different strings move with differing velocity. A higher or deeper note resounds depending on the speed... and the sounding together of these different notes yields harmony. The person who has risen to the degree of clairaudience in Devachan hears the motions of the heavenly bodies... in exactly the same way. Through the ratios of the different velocities of the planets arise the fundamental notes of the harmony of the spheres which resounds through the universe. In the Pythagorean school a harmony of the spheres was thus spoken of justifiably: it can be heard with spiritual ears.

If you take a thin sheet of brass and cover it with uniformly graded sand and then draw a violin bow across the edge, the sand arranges itself in quite clear lines... The sound effects a distribution of physical substance; such figures are called Chladni sound patterns. When the spiritual sound of the music of the spheres resounded through the universe, it arranged the planets and their relationships in this way. What you see in the universe, that was arranged by this creative sound of the Godhead.'

10. See R. Steiner, lecture Dornach, 22.2.24 in GA 278.
11. See R. Steiner, lecture Dornach, 20.2.24 in GA 278.
12. See R. Steiner, lecture Stuttgart, 8.3.23 in GA 283.

13. Lothar Vogel, *Der dreigliedrige Mensch*, chap. 3 Das Knochensystem, Dornach, Philosophisch-Anthroposophischer Verlag, 2nd edition 1979:

'The principle of development of the bones of the limbs:... is incorporated from the forces of the periphery. In the embryonic development of the skeleton, we find that indeed the bones of the limbs do come into being from the periphery and grow towards the centre, towards the torso. Initially comes the raying of fingers and toes, then of the middle of the hand and the middle of the foot, and of the arms and legs; and relatively late the upper arm and thigh into the shoulder and pelvis.'

14. See R. Steiner, *The Renewal of Education* (lecture Basel, 21.4.20), Steiner Schools Fellowship. GA 301.
15. See Friedrich Schiller, *Letters on the Aesthetic Education of Man*, OUP, 1967.
16. See R. Steiner, lecture Dornach 21 and 23.2.24 in GA 278.
17. On the musical experience of the Lemurians in ninths, the Atlanteans in sevenths, the post-Atlanteans in fifths, and our age in thirds, see R. Steiner, *The Driving Force of Spiritual Powers in World History* (lecture Dornach 16.3.23), Steiner Book Centre, Toronto, Canada, 1972. GA 222. (Translators' note: further research on tonal systems, see H. Pfrogner, *Lebendige Tonwelt*, München, Langen Muller 1976 and H. Ruland, *Ein Weg zur Erweiterung des Tonerlebens*, Verlag die Pforte, Basel 1981 English translation: 'Expanding Tonal Awareness', RSP, forthcoming 1992.)
18. R. Steiner, 'Die Apokalypse' [The Apocalypse], (lecture Munich 8.5.07) in the supplement to *Das Goetheanum*, 1945, 22nd year, no. 19:

'In the ancient Pythagorean schools numbers played an important role... When we think of the numbers as being heard by the ear of the spirit, then we have the music of the spheres. The harmonies alone were expressed in numbers... The four members of man's being, as depicted by the Pythagorean, harmonize in ratios of 1:3:7:12. This signifies that sound in which the four numbers harmonize as do the four members of the human being: 1 – the ego, 3 – called the 'Mothers'. The three notes: 1st by the note from the sun, 2nd by the moon, 3rd the note of the earth itself – on to the astral body... What proceeds from the earth, the sun and the moon harmonizes in our astral body.'

19. See R. Steiner, *The Wisdom of Man* (lecture Berlin, 26.10.09) AP New York, 1971. GA 115.
20. R. Steiner, *Lectures to Teachers* (lecture Dornach, 5.1.22, answers to questions) Anthroposophical Publishing Co., London 1948.
    Also published in R. Steiner, *Soul Economy and Waldorf Education* RSP/AP London 1986. GA 303:

'The intensive experience of melody would consist in becoming used to perceiving the note, which is taken today as *one* note, as a kind of melody.'

See also R. Steiner, lecture Dornach, 16.3.23 in GA 283.

R. Steiner, lecture Dornach, 21.2.24 in GA 278:

'We have to... become aware of the melody, not the chord in the single note,... A number of notes are contained in the single note, every note consisting of three notes' (present, memory, expectation).

[For further discussion on this, according to Steiner, purely inner, supersensible experience, see Ruland, *Ein Weg, zur Erweiterung des Tonerlebnis*, Basel 1981 ('Expanding Tonal Awareness', forthcoming RSP 1992), and *Die Neugehurt der Musik aus den Wesen des Menschen*, Schaffhausen 1987 ('The rebirth of music from within man'), and a further article in *Resonanz* no 8, 1988. Translators' note.]

21. See R. Steiner, lecture Dornach, 23.2.24 in GA 278.
22. See R. Steiner, lecture Dornach, 21.2.24 in GA 278.
23. Cf. R. Steiner, *Theosophy*, RSP London 1975. GA 9.
24. See R. Steiner, *Verses and Meditations*, RSP London 1972 and R. Steiner, *Truth-Wrought Words*, AP New York 1979. GA 40.
25. See R. Steiner, lectures Dornach, 19 and 20.2.24 in GA 278. See also R. Steiner, lecture Berlin, 3.2.10 in *Metamorphosen des Seelenlebens*, ('Metamorphosis of soul-experience'), Dornach 1984.

R. Steiner, lecture Berlin 12.11.06, in GA 283:

'The combined efforts of sentient soul and sentient body are of special significance for the musical element. We have to understand that all consciousness arises from a kind of overcoming of the outer world. What comes to consciousness in man as pleasure or joy signifies victory of the spiritual over the mere bodily, living element... It is possible for the human being who returns from sleep with the inner vibrations to intensify the notes and perceive the victory of the sentient soul over the sentient body, so that the soul is capable of feeling stronger than the body. With the effects of the minor mode we can always perceive how the vibrations of the sentient body are stronger, whereas with the major mode the sentient soul vibrates more strongly and predominates over the sentient body.'

R. Steiner, lecture Cologne 3.12.06, in GA 283:

'The etheric body is an etheric archetype of the physical body. A much more delicate body which is related to the etheric body and inclines to the astral realm, is the sentient body... The sentient soul is as though incorporated into the sentient body; it is placed within the sentient body. Just as a sword in its scabbard forms a whole, so the sentient body and the sentient soul represent a whole... When the human being sleeps the sentient body remains in bed with the physical and etheric bodies, but the higher soul members including the sentient soul dwell in the world of Devachan... In as much as man lives and weaves in the world of flowing sounds, he himself is flooded by these sounds. When he returns from this Devachanic world, his own consciousness soul, intellectual soul and sentient soul are permeated with the vibrations of the Devachanic realm; he has them within himself. With them he enters into the physical world. Having absorbed these vibrations of Devachan along with him, the human being can convey them out of the sentient soul back to the sentient body and the ether body. Because he carries the vibrations with him out of Devachan, the human being can carry them over to his etheric body...

During the night the human being fetches from the world of flowing sounds the strength to carry it over to the sentient body and etheric body. A person creates music or perceives music because he already possesses these sounds in his sentient body. Although the human being is unaware of having absorbed sounds during the night, when he awakens in the morning he nevertheless senses these imprints of the spiritual world when he listens to music. When he hears music, a clairvoyant can see how the notes flow, how they seize the more solid substance of the etheric body and cause it to reverberate; from this the person experiences pleasure. The reason for this is that he feels like a victor over his etheric body by means of his astral body... In the case of certain musical sounds something of the astral body flows into the etheric body. The latter has now received new notes. A kind of struggle arises between the sentient body and the etheric body. If these notes are so strong that they overcome the ether body's own notes, then cheerful music in the major mode results. When music in the major mode has an effect then we can follow how the sentient body is victor over the etheric body. In the case of the minor mode the etheric body is victor over the sentient body. The etheric body opposes the vibrations of the sentient body.'

R. Steiner, (lecture Leipzig, 10.11.06) in GA 283:

'With a musician... the Devachanic world resounds into our earthly world. Music is the expression of the sounds in Devachan... The image of the sounds in Devachan exists in the etheric body of man. The etheric body, which the human being has so fashioned in himself, is penetrated with the vibrations of the Devachanic world. This metamorphosed etheric body of the human being is embedded in the lower (etheric body). And this new etheric body goes on vibrating and thus the feeling arises of overcoming the lower etheric body by the higher. When the feeling of overcoming the lower etheric body by the higher arises, the major mode resounds. When the higher etheric body cannot become master over the unpurified one, it feels as if the minor mode resounds from without. The human being comes to know the mastery of his feelings through the major mode. If he feels that the high vibration cannot penetrate, then he senses the minor mode.'

From *'Goethes Tonlehre'* ('Goethe's theory of music'), compiled by Max Schuurman in *'Goethes Verhaltnis zur Tonkunst'* in *Das Goetheanum*, 1932, 11th year, no. 32:

'The major and minor modes show the polarity in the theory of sound. First principle of both. The major mood arises through ascent, through an acceleration upwards, through an extension of all the intervals upwards. The minor mood arises from descending, precipitating downwards, extension of the intervals downwards. (The ascending minor scale has to turn itself into the major.) – Exposition of this antithesis is as the foundation of all music.'

Goethe, letter of Ch. Schlosser 19.2.1815, in Heinrich Duntzer *Aus Goethes Freundeskreise*, Braunschweig 1868. Also in Max Schuurman, 'Goethe und das Dur-Mollproblem.' *Das Goetheanum*, 1933, 12th year, no.1:

'I am convinced of this: As the major mood arises from the extension of the monad, so it practises an equivalent effect on man's nature; this it urges into the object, into activity, into the widths, towards the periphery. The matter is similar for the minor mood. Because this arises from the contraction of the monad, it contracts too, concentrates, urges into the subject and knows how to find there the last hiding-place in which it is wont to conceal the most precious melancholy.

According to this antithesis military marches, indeed everything summoning and challenging, has to be fashioned in the major mode. The minor mood, on the other hand, is not solely dedicated to pain or sadness, but it also produces every kind of concentration. Polonaises should be written in this mode, not merely because these dances were originally written according to its dramatic character, but because the party of dancers which here represents the subject, concentrates, likes to weave together, the dancers lingering and passing by each other. Liveliest dances alternate very wisely between major and minor. Here diastole and systole bring out the pleasant feeling of inhalation in the human being; on the other hand I have never known anything as terrible as a military march in the minor mood. Here both poles inwardly oppose each other and wring the heart instead of making it neutral.'

A further remark from Goethe, (ibid.):

'The foundation of what is known as the minor lies within the monad of music itself. I deeply believe this. Perhaps the following will pave a way for more detailed development. When the monad expands, the major arises; when it contracts, the minor comes into existence. I have expressed this generation in the diagram, where the notes are viewed as a series, through ascent and descent. Both forms allow themselves to be united when you take the inaudible, deepest note as the most inward centre of the monad, the inaudible, highest as the periphery of the same.'

26. R. Steiner, *Spiritual Science and Medicine* lecture Dornach, 22.3.20) RSP London, 1948. GA 312:

'In the last resort the heart is an organ of perception... Thus, as you perceive with your eyes the external colours, you perceive through your heart (though in a dull subconsciousness) through your heart what goes on in your abdomen. Ultimately the heart is a sense organ for inner perception.'

R. Steiner, *Rhythmen im Kosmos und in Menschenwesen* [MS trans. 'Seven Lectures to Workmen' R. Steiner Library, London] (lecture Dornach, 6.6.23). GA 350:

'The heart is not intended to pump the blood through the body, but it is a sense organ which perceives everything, like the whole head does... The head perceives the whole blood circulation by means of the heart... The heart perceives the movements of the whole human being. Through this the heart is set into motion. The heart is set into motion by movements produced by hunger for air and hunger for food. In the movements of the heart we notice whether our body is in good order or not... The head is constantly doing what we do when we take a patient's pulse. Through the heart, the head constantly senses the whole of the blood circulation. Indeed, the head feels through the heart whatever goes on in the body.'

Lothar Vogel, *Der dreigliedrige Mensch*, chap. 6: Der rhythmische Organismus. Philosophisch-Anthroposophischer Verlag, Dornach, 2nd edition, 1979:

'This task of the heart, ... as a sense organ, is to perceive the needs of all the organs in activity and passivity; in systole and diastole, to allow the forces of destiny to influence organic evolution.'

27. See R. Steiner, lectures Dornach, 22 and 26.2.24 in GA 278.
Throughout the course the emphasis is on feeling, sensing and ensouling.

26.2.24:

'Whoever cannot enter in feeling at a specific place will not find the right point of departure... Without this permeation of the movements with feeling, musical eurythmy utterly loses its meaning.'

28. See R. Steiner, lectures Stuttgart, 7 and 8.3.23 in GA 283.
29. See R. Steiner, lecture Dornach, 19.2.24 in GA 278.
30. See R. Steiner, *Art as seen in the Light of Mystery Wisdom* (lecture Dornach, 28.12.14) RSP London, 1984. GA 275.
31. See ibid. (lecture Dornach, 29.12.14) GA 275.
32. See R. Steiner *Kunst und Kunsterkenntnis* [Art and its appreciation] lecture Dornach, 12.9.20. GA 271.
R. Steiner *Meditatively Acquired Knowledge of Man* (lecture Stuttgart 21.9.20) Steiner Schools Fellowship, 1982. GA 302a.

16.9.20:

'Were we not to have music, really frightening forces would rise up in the human being... Music is the means of defence against the Luciferic forces rising up out of the inwardness of man: 'treasons, stratagems and spoils' (Shakespeare: Lorenzo in *The Merchant of Venice*, V,1) and it is not for nothing that the world contains the element of music and speech, quite apart from the pleasure it affords man. This element is there in order to make the human being Human.'

On musical perception, understanding and memory see R. Steiner 'The supersensible origin of art', lecture Dornach, 12.9.20. GA 271:

'You know that this astral body which we bear within us only exists for a time after death, then we discard it. However, this astral body contains the real musical element... When we now arrive at the stage after death where we discard our astral body, then we also discard everything which is musical that reminds us of this earthly life. However, at this cosmic moment the musical element is transformed into the music of the spheres... After death we discard our astral body: then (pardon the banal expression) everything musical in us switches over into the music of the spheres. Thus in music and poetry we have an antecedent of what our world, our existence is after death.'

R. Steiner, *Art in the Light of Mystery Wisdom* (lecture Dornach, 12.9.20) RSP, London 1970. GA 271:

'We bring about a possibility that the human being in his next life will be better constituted if, in the kama loca time after death, when he still has his astral body, he can still have many memories of musical events. The musical element is maintained so long as the astral body is maintained.'

33. Hendrika Hollenback, *'Die ersten Anfange der Toneurythmie'* ['The first beginnings of music eurythmy'] in the supplement to *Das Goetheanum*, 1948, 25th year, no. 38:

'It was a fine moment for me when Rudolf Steiner confirmed something for which I had been searching for a long time and thought I had found, namely the connection between the notes, the gestures of musical eurythmy and the planets. As long as I had searched on the basis of our present day planetary system I was not able to find the connection, until one day it finally dawned on me that it was cosmic evolution with which I had to relate the notes. Suddenly new light shone on to the movements of music eurythmy. For just as the arms move downwards in the three stops of the major remaining with F and G in middle position, and then proceed upwards again, so does our earthly evolution proceed through Saturn, Sun and Moon up to the earthly development which is divided into the stages of the Mars and Mercury evolution. The same holding of the arms in F and G suddenly stood in a new light and the lifting of yourself over earthly gravity through the little jumps in G-A-B appeared accordingly in the sense of rendering the upwards evolution, where through the upwards reaching of the arms the octave is attained. As is the Vulcan stage, the stage of spirit-man, as through Jupiter and Venus evolution... I was deeply satisfied when I went to Dr Steiner with a small sketch where I had arranged eurythmic gestures, planetary signs and names of notes. He looked it over then said: "Yes, it is correct.".'

See also note 7.

34. See R. Steiner (lecture Stuttgart, 7.3.23) GA 283.
35. See footnotes 12, 30 and 31.
36. See footnotes 12 and 17.
37. R. Steiner, *Die Entstehung und die Entwicklung der Eurythmy* ['The origins and development of eurythmy'] (lecture Dornach, 23.8.15). GA 277a:

'The spoken word appears on the human being. Musical sound appears through the whole human being.'

38. See R. Steiner, lecture 2.12.22 in GA 283.

39. R. Steiner, *Art as seen in the Light of Mystery Wisdom* (lecture Dornach 1.1.15), RSP London 1984:

'The world of music will deepen and enliven human soul life in a very similar way. During the era that is now drawing to a close, the essential thing is that a person experiences a note as such, and then the relationship of one note to another. In future people will be able to experience what is behind the note.

The note will be regarded as a kind of window through which people will enter the spiritual world, and then it will not depend on this vague feeling of how one note is added to the next, to form melodies for example, but behind the single note the soul will experience a moral-spiritual quality right through the note. The soul will penetrate right into the spiritual world as through a window. The secrets of the individual note will be discovered behind the actual note through this experience of it.

We are still a long way from this feeling of being able to step into the spiritual world from the sense world through every single note. But this will come. We shall experience the note as an opening made by the gods from the spiritual world yonder to this physical, sense-perceptible world, and through the note climb out of the physical world into the spiritual world. Through the prime for example, which we sense as an absolute, and not in reference to earlier notes of the scale, we shall feel how we climb out of the sense-perceptible world into the spiritual world and we sense the danger in this. We are threatened on entry with being taken captive, that the prime wishes to suck us in most horribly through the window and make us completely disappear into the spiritual world... When we climb out of the physical world into the spiritual world through the window of the second, we shall have the impression of powers there in the spiritual world that, as it were, take pity on our weakness... We enter a completely silent world when we enter the spiritual world through the absolute prime. If we enter through the second we come to a world where, if we pay attention, various gentle high-pitched notes resound wanting to comfort us in our weakness... In the spiritual world we have to take the notes with us and identify with them, live completely over there on the other side of the membrane that separates us from the physical, sense-perceptible world, and in which we have to imagine the windows, which are the notes.

If we enter the spiritual world through the third, we have the feeling of an even greater weakness. If we enter the spiritual world in this way, we shall feel that we are really very weak in the physical, sense-perceptible world, where its spiritual content is concerned. But with regard to the third (and remember we have become sound, we ourselves are a third) we shall feel that there are friends over there who, although they themselves are not thirds, approach us according to the kind of disposition we had in the physical, sense-perceptible world... People who want to become composers will have to enter especially through the third for there the tonal progressions will be found, musical compositions that will stimulate their artistic creativity...

When we penetrate through the fourth into the spiritual world we will have a remarkable experience that now although no new notes appear from any direction, those that have come before when we were experiencing the third, will easily exist in the soul as memories. And we find that in continuing to live with these tonal memories they perpetually take on ever different colourings, when we are penetrated through the fourth into the spiritual world. These memories are now as bright and cheerful as can be, then they sink down to the silence of the grave. The modulating of the voice, the ascending and descending of the notes, in short, the progress in the mood of a composition will be given along this path, through these tonal memories.

The fifth will produce more subjective experiences that effect stimulation and enrichment of the experience of the soul. It has the effect of a magic wand which conjures up the secrets of the tonal world yonder from unfathomable depths... And then above all something will appear like an inward experience of those powers which, for example, guide man from one incarnation to the next.'

40. R. Steiner, *True and False Paths of Spiritual Investigation*, (lecture Torquay 22.8.24) RSP/AP, London 1969. GA 243:

'Now in general terms there was a current in human evolution which had a specific inclination towards the sculptural, pictorial arts... For centuries another impulse has developed and this is the impulse towards the art of music. For this reason the pictorial arts are also taking on a more or less musical form. In the artistic sphere the musical element belongs to the future of humanity and this includes everything of a musical nature that can also appear in the other performing arts.

The Goetheanum building at Dornach was a creation related to the musical element. This is why its architecture, sculpture and painting have been so little understood up to now. Also the building which is now to be erected will be difficult to understand because the musical element must be led over into the elements of painting and sculpture if it is to be in keeping with the evolution of humanity.

But just that... which is the highest summit of human evolution, the approaching figure of the Christ, indeed the vital, spiritually-vital figure of the Christ, is something which in a certain sense has succeeded wonderfully in painting... but must in future be reached through the musical element... The musical element is capable of placing before the world this Christ-Impulse in music, in formed, ensouled and spiritually permeated sounds. If music allows itself to be inspired by anthroposophical spiritual science, it will find the way in the purely artistic sphere to solve with feeling the riddle of how to bring to life symphonically in sound what lives as the Christ-Impulse in the universe and the earth.

Taking the area of the third in the major, we need only try to deepen the musical experience of it, bringing it inwardly as far as a mystical feeling. If you experience this area as something totally enclosed musically within the inner being of man, if you sense the area of the fifth in major as something of a protecting mantle where man, entering into this formation of the fifth, reaches the boundary between the human and the cosmic realm where the cosmos resounds into the human being and the human being yearns out towards the cosmos (indeed, storms out towards it with yearning), then by means of the mystery which plays between the area of the third and that of the fifth in the major, you will experience precisely in the musical realm what as an inner human element wants to reach out into the cosmos.

Discords of the seventh express what man, sensing in the cosmos, can experience when he is on the way to the various regions of the spirit. And if you then succeed in letting the discords of the seventh fade in such a way that by their fading they acquire a certain definition, then these discords of the seventh, as they vanish, acquire what can be expressed as a "musical firmament" to the musical experience.

Having already had the subtle intimation of a minor experience in the major experience, having found in the vanishing of the discords of the seventh, in the self-creation of the discords of the seventh a totality that almost becomes harmonious, almost concordant because it is vanishing, having found the possibility of emerging in an intense minor mood from the discords of the seventh, having found your way back into the realm of the fifth in the minor, out of the vanishing of the discords of the seventh almost into harmony, having found the way back into the realm of the fifth in the minor and having thence succeeded in permeating the area of the fifth with the area of the minor third, then on this path you will have achieved an experience, a musical experience of the incarnation, indeed that of the incarnation of Christ.

In this "feeling-yourself-outside" into what appears, unlike what is felt cosmically, to be the discordant area of the seventh which you transform into a firmament by letting the octave stand behind it, but only approximately; having taken hold of this feeling, you then return in the way indicated and find how in the germinal form of the concord of the third in the minor there lies the possibility to represent the Incarnation as something musical; then, when you go back to the major in this region, the "Halleluja" of Christ will be allowed to resound in a purely musical way out of the formation of the sounds.

Then the human being will represent within the forming of the sounds something directly supersensible for musical feeling... And so it can come about (it only depends on people) that the Christ-Impulse in its true form can come to manifestation precisely in the sphere of music.'

[Translators' note: see H. Beckh, *Das Parsifal Christus-Erlebnis*, Die Christengemeinschaft: Stuttgart 1930, where a connection between the above intervals and Wagner's theme is indicated in two footnotes. English translation in manuscript: 'The Parsifal Christ-experience'.]

41. R. Steiner, *Der Baum des Lebens und der Baum der Erkentnis des Guten und Bosen* [The Tree of Life and the Tree of Knowledge of Good and Evil] (lecture Dornach 31.7.15). GA 162:

'The basic mood of this new world-conception (since the Mystery of Golgotha) is musical, the basic mood of the old world is sculptural. The basic mood of the new age is really musical, and the world will become ever more musical. In order to continue rightly on the path of human evolution, we must know the importance of striving towards a musical element and not repeating the old sculptural one. I have frequently mentioned that in an important place in our building (the First Goetheanum) a figure of archetypal man will be set up, which we can also speak of as the Christ, and which will have Lucifer on the one side and Ahriman on the other. What is concentrated in the Christ we extract and divide up again between Lucifer and Ahriman — in so far as it can be divided up. What is welded into one figure, we perform musically, in that we make it into a kind of melody: Christ-Lucifer-Ahriman. Our building really is formed according to this principle... It bears the special basic imprint in itself of bringing the sculptural forms into musical movement.'

R. Steiner, *Ways to a New Style in Architecture*, (lecture Dornach 17.6.14), Anthroposophical Publishing Co., London 1927. GA 286:

'Art is the introducing of organs through which the gods are able to speak to mankind...our building is to speak through its interior forms, but it must be the language of the gods...the house of speech, the speaking house.'

42. R. Steiner, *Man and the World of Stars and the Spirtiual Communion of Mankind* (lecture Dornach 17.6.14), AP, New York: 1963. GA 219:

'If human beings were only to develop spatial knowledge and not spiritualize it, if they were to remain in anthropology and not be willing to advance to anthroposophy, then the Michael Age would pass by. Michael would retire from his rulership, carrying to the gods his message that humanity wants to be separated from the gods. If Michael is to carry the right message to the world of the gods then he will have to say: During my age human beings have raised to a supersensible form what they have developed apart from the divine-spiritual world by way of pure spatial notions and we are able in return to accept human beings, for they have united their thinking, their concepts, with our thinking, our concepts. Yes, Michael will not have to say to the gods, if human beings want to pursue their proper development: Men have become accustomed only to goggle at everything they see in space, they have learnt to despise what lives in them alone. Instead he will say if human beings are resolved to reach the goal of their earthly existence: Men have endeavoured to carry what lives in time, in the supersensible, once again into space. Therefore, since human beings are not merely content to gape at what they see in space and since they do not merely want to accept such coarsening as is favoured at the beginning of the twentieth century, their existence can once again be linked directly to the life of the gods.

When we really pursue anthroposophy out of the spirit of initiation science, it means we have to interest ourselves in cosmic concerns, in something with which humanity has to be concerned in unison with the divine world. And in modern times this comprises a very great deal. It is a matter of whether we wish to sow the seed of what the right, further co-existence with the divine-spiritual world is, or whether we do not wish to sow this seed.'

Further reading:

R. Steiner

1908	*Universe, Earth and Man*, R. Steiner Publishing Co.: London 1955, GA 105.
1911/12	*The World of the Senses and the Spirit*, (lecture Hannover 1.1.12) R. Steiner Publishing Co.: London 1947. GA 134.
1914	*Christ and the Human Soul*, (lecture Norrköpping 16.7.14, RSP: London 1972. GA 155.
1923	*The Child's Changing Consciousness and Waldorf Education*, RSP: London, and New York: AP, 1988. GA 306.
1924	*Essentials of Education*, RSP: London 1968. GA308.

Other Authors:

Karl von Baltz, *Rudolf Steiners musikalische Impulse*. 2.Aufl., Philosophisch-Anthroposophischer Verlag, Dornach 1981. ['R. Steiner's musical stimuli']

Hermann Beckh, *Vom geistigen Wesen der Tonarten*. 2.Aufl., Preuss und Jäger, Breslau 1925. ['Music's Secret Zodiac', The Robinswood Press: Stourbridge. Forthcoming.]
Die Sprache der Tonarten in der Musik von Bach bis Bruckner, Urachhaus: Stuttgart 1977. [Translation in manuscript 'The language of tonality'].

Wilhelm Dorfler, *Das Lebensgefüge der Musik*, Band I Philosophisch-Anthroposophischer Verlag: Dornach 1975. ['Music's vital structure' Vol. 1.]

Armin J. Husemann, *Der musikalische Bau des Menschen*, Freies Geistesleben, Stuttgart 1989 ['The musical structure of the human being', Floris books: Edinburgh. Forthcoming].

Ralph und Willi Kux, *Erinnerungen an Rudolf Steiner. Eurythmie und Musik*. Mellinger: Stuttgart 1976. [Translation in manuscript: 'Recollections of R. Steiner, and eurythmy and music.']

Anni Von Lange, *Mensch, Musik und Kosmos*. Novalis: Freiburg i. Br. 1956. ['Man, music and cosmos.' Forthcoming, RSP]

Hans Erhard Lauer, *Musik und Musiker in anthroposophischer Betrachtung*. Selbstverlag: Wien 1933. ['Music and Musicians – an anthroposophical perspective.']
'The Evolution of music Through Changes in Tone-Systems' in *Cosmic Music: musical Keys to the Interpretation of Reality* edited by J. Godwin, Inner Traditions: Rochester, Vermont 1989.

Lea van der Pals and Annemarie Bäschlin, *Ton-Heileurythmie*, Dornach 1991. ['Therapeutic Music Eurythmy', The Robinswood Press: Stourbridge. Forthcoming 1992].

Hermann Pfrogner, *Musik. Geschichte ihrer Deutung*. Karl Alber: Freiburg/München 1954. ['A history of views on music']
Lebendige Tonwelt. Zum Phänomen Musik. Langen/Muller: München/Wien 1981. ['The living world of music']
Die sieben Lebensprozesse. Eine musiktherapeutische Anregung. Die Kommenden: Freiburg 1978. ['The seven life-processes. Theraputic suggestions']

Bibliographic Survey

Works by R. Steiner mentioned in the appendix. GA (Gesamtausgabe = Bibliographic Survey) numbers, published in Dornach, Switzerland unless otherwise stated. The dates refer either to when the lectures were given, or with written books, to the first edition.

GA 9	Theosophie. (1904)
GA 13	Die Geheimwissenschaft im Umriss. (1909)
GA 36	Das Goetheanum in seinen zehn Jahren. Goethe und Goetheanum.
GA 40	Wahrspruchworte.
GA 58	Pfade der Seelenerlebnisse Metamophosen des Seelenlebens.
GA 102	Das Hereinwirken geistiger Wesenheiten in den Menschen. (1908)
GA 105	Welt Erde und Mensch, deren Wesen und Entwickelung. (1908)
GA 115	Anthroposophie, Psychosophie, Pneumatosophie. (1909)
GA 124	Exkurse in das Gebiet des Markus-Evangeliums.
GA 134	Die Welt der Sinne und die Welt des Geistes. (1911/12)
GA 155	Christus und die menschliche Seele. (1914)
GA 208	Anthroposophie als Kosmosophie. (1921)
GA 218	Geistige Zusammenhänge in der Gestaltung des menschlichen Organismus. (1922)
GA 219	Das Verhältnis der Sternenwelt zum Menschen und des Menschen zur Sternenwelt. Die geistige Kommunion der Menschheit. (1922)
GA 222	Die Impulsierung des weltgeschichtlichen Geschehens durch geistige Mächte. (1923)
GA 243	Das Initiaten-Bewusstsein. (1924)
GA 271	Kunst und Kunsterkenntnis. (1918)
GA 275	Kunst im Lichte der Mysterienweisheit. (1914)
GA 276	Das Künstlerische in seiner Weltmission. (1923)
GA 277a	Die Entstehung und die Entwickelung der Eurythmie. (1967)
GA 278	Eurythmie als sichtbarer Gesang. (1924)
GA 283	Das Wesen des Musikalischen und das Tonerlebnis im Menschen. (1906/1922/1923)
GA 286	Wege zu einem neuen Baustil, Stuttgart: Verlag Freies Geistesleben. (1924)
GA 301	Die Erneuerung der pädagogisch-didaktischen Kunst durch Geisteswissenschaft. (1920)
GA 302a	Erziehung und Unterricht aus Menschenerkenntnis. (1920)
GA 303	Die gesunde Entwickelung des Leiblich-Physischen als Grundlage der Freien Entfaltung des Seelisch-Geistigen. (1922)
GA 306	Die pädagogische Praxis vom Gesichtspunkte geisteswissenschaftlicher Menschenerkenntnis. (1923)
GA 312	Geisteswissenschaft und Medizin. (1920)
GA 320	Geisteswissenschaftliche Impulse zur Entwickelung der Physik I. (1919)
GA 350	Rhythmen im Kosmos und im Menschenwesen. (1923)
	Der Baum des Lebens und der Baum der Erkenntnis des Guten und Bösen. (1915)

An Appendix in the German edition of GA 283 offers a comprehensive list of the places in Steiner's works which refer to music.